A TREATISE OF THE
COMPENDIUM

BY

REV. G. H. KERSTEN

INHERITANCE PUBLISHING CO.
Grand Rapids, Michigan

An accompanying workbook based on this volume, entitled Introductory Bible Doctrine Course *by Rev. J.R. Beeke and J.W. Beeke, is available from Netherlands Reformed Book and Publishing Committee, c/o B. Harskamp, 1020 N. Main Ave., Sioux Center, Iowa 51250.*

Printed in the United States of America

Reprinted, November 1989

Preface

Our Synod of 1956 decided to have the explanation of our "Compendium", written by the late Rev. G. H. Kersten, translated for publication in the English language.

It is our sincere desire that the King of kings will graciously bless these efforts to the end that our younger generations may gain a clearer insight into our doctrine which is based on the Word of God.

May the Holy Spirit bless it to the hearts of many, to the salvation of their souls and that the triune God may receive the honor and the glory.

In the name of our Congregations,

REV. W. C. LAMAIN.

Contents

Introduction

Before I begin the Exposition of the Compendium, I would like to say a word about the Doctrinal Standards of The Netherlands Reformed Church.

(a) In these Standards the church expresses those things, which, being founded on the Word of God, it believes.

The church does this to acquaint itself to the world. Therefore these Standards have been called, "Symbols of the Reformed Church," i.e., marks of recognition — passwords. It was for this purpose particularly that the 37 Articles of our Confession of Faith were drawn up.

(b) These Standards serve to propagate the knowledge of faith, with the youth as well as with adults. This was the object of composing the Catechism.

(c) The church expresses itself by means of these Standards to preserve the Unity of the Faith, and defend itself against heresies as they appear. In this respect we think especially of the Five Articles Against the Remonstrants, commonly known as the Canons of Dort."

This threefold object lies behind each of our Doctrinal Standards. Therefore they have also been called, "The Forms of Unity."

The Forms of Unity of The Netherlands' churches are:

1. *The Netherlands Confession of Faith.*
2. *The Heidelberg Catechism.*
3. *The Canons of Dort.*

These Forms are accepted by all of Reformed persuasion, not on an equal plane with, but subordinate to, the Word of God; whereas they who deviate from the truth, oppose these Forms and their church authority.

Let us consider for a moment the origin of these Doctrinal Standards, from an historical viewpoint.

I. THE CONFESSION OF FAITH

This Confession was composed by Guido de Bres, who was born in the year 1522, in Mons de Hainault. Already in his youth he was wont to read the Holy Scripture, and it pleased the Lord to use this as the means of his conversion. The persecution of those days caused him to flee to England, which country, under

the leadership of Edward VI, offered asylum to many exiles of
the faith. Here de Bres matured, under the guidance of a Lasco.
When Mary ascended the throne in England, and bloody persecution was resumed again, also in that country, de Bres returned to
his fatherland. He served as an itinerant minister here from 1552
until 1556. He traveled out of Lisle, which he made the center of
his labors, and where the congregation became very flourishing.
A dreadful persecution induced de Bres to flee in 1556, and practically ruined the whole congregation. In Frankfort on the
Main, where he sought refuge, he again met a Lasco, and also
Calvin. After spending some time also in Lousanne and Geneva,
he returned to The Netherlands in 1559, and lived in Tournay;
but here also a wave of persecution broke loose.

De Bres protested against this in the following manner:

In the night of Nov. 1, 1561, a package was thrown over the
wall of the castle at Tournay. Besides a protest, this package also
contained the Confession of Faith. This was done in confutation
of the many false accusations which were levelled against the
Reformed doctrine. In the same year, 1561, the Confession of
Faith was published, probably by J. Crespin, at Geneva.

De Bres fled to France, and resided in Amiens. In 1565 he was
minister at Sedan, but the following year he returned to The
Netherlands. After staying in Antwerp for a time, he established
himself in Valenciennes, France. Here he received the support
of a Rev. Le Grange. The preaching of these two ministers bore
much fruit. Rome was not inactive however, and soon Noir
Carnes, a Spanish officer, lay siege to the city. When these ministers sought to escape, they were captured, and, after being subjected to extreme torture, they were hanged, on May 31, 1567.
Although Guido deBres was not permitted by his executioners
to pray at the foot of the ladder, yet the enemy could not prevent
his entrance into glory, where his soul now sings praises before
the throne of God. The blood of the martyrs calls loudly for the
day of vengeance upon Rome.

The Confession of Faith was now subjected to the judgment of
such renowned ministers as Petrus Dathenus and Casper v.d.
Heijden, and also to that of the consistory of Antwerp. It received unanimous approval. The Convent of Wezel, and the con-

sequent Synods, required the signing of the ministers, and later also of the professors; even the school teachers had to affix their signatures to the Confession of Faith.

The National Synod, held at Dordrecht, in the years 1618-1619, also discussed this Confession, on the insistence of the civil authorities, with the result that all the theologians, including those delegated from foreign countries, judged it to be in full accord with God's Word.

How fitting therefore for us to hold this Confession in high esteem, and especially so in times when the truth is fallen in the street. Read oft therein in your searchings of Scripture; and may the Lord sanctify it to your souls.

II. The Heidelberg Catechism

The Catechism used in the churches of The Netherlands and also in our churches in this country was compiled in Heidelberg, the capital of the Electorate of the Palatinate; hence the name "Heidelberg Catechism." The drawing up of this Catechism was decided upon (in The Palatinate) after a heavy conflict had been engaged in by the Lutherans and the Calvinists. This struggle reached its climax when Prince Otto, who had no masculine heir, wanted to have a mausoleum erected for himself in the church, and adorn the same with sculpture. The Lutherans gave their approval, but the Calvinists could not agree to it. Had they been successful in abolishing statues and images from the church, to permit their return in this way? Never!

Prince Otto died, and Frederick III became his successor. This God-fearing Prince, who not only had the welfare of the country at heart, but was also deeply concerned about the future of the true religion, arranged a debate between delegates of the Lutherans and Calvinists. The Lutherans now had an opportunity to defend their doctrine, but their defeat was so decisive, that one even of their champions turned to the Reformed religion. Now the case (of The Palatinate) was conclusively settled. Two youthful theologians were appointed by Frederick III to compile a Catechism to be taught in the churches and schools.

These two theologians were:

Zacharias Ursinus, born on July 18, 1534, and,
Caspar Olevianus, born on Aug. 10, 1536.

The one therefore was 28 years old, and the other 26, when this commission of so great importance was conferred upon them. With what heavenly light were these young men illuminated, and what a rich blessing rested upon their labors, to the comfort of God's dear people.

This Catechism was approved in 1563 by the Heidelberg Synod, and Frederick III wrote the introduction to it himself, on January 19, 1563. In the second edition, which was published a few weeks after the first, the 80th question was added, at the request of Calvin, teaching the vast difference between the Lord's Supper and the Popish Mass. The Catechism was first divided into Lord's Days in the fourth edition, which was also published in 1563, the same year as previous editions. Overnight, as it were, the Heidelberg Catechism was spread over all Germany; it was being translated into all European languages; even into the Greek and Hebrew.

The enemy stood amazed. Recovering from the first shock, they quickly concentrated all their forces of strategy to exterminate this despised Catechism. At the Diet of Augsburg, held in 1566, they bent every effort to win the victory. This was the same Diet before which Frederick III was summoned to appear. With Roman Catholics, Lutherans, and the Kaiser with his vassals, all conspiring against him, the sentence against the pious Frederick III was a foregone conclusion.

The outlook, from the human standpoint, was indeed very dark. The Electors Frederick of Saxony and Herman Van Keulen, had already lost their political standing and property; so what future now awaited Frederick (of the Palatinate)? Still this Elector was determined to go, and nothing could influence him to alter his decision to appear before this Diet. Earthly possessions were not his greatest asset, and if any deprived him of his life, he would the sooner enter into glory. So wrote this God-fearing Elector. What a testimony! When encountering great dangers, grace alone will enable one to speak thus.

With his second eldest son, John Casimir, whom he called his spiritual armorbearer, Frederick III started out. He was comforted by his childlike faith in God's promises, and declared openly before Emperor and Princes, "My Lord and Saviour Jesus Christ hath given unto me and all His faithful the sure promises, that everything which I forsake for His Name's sake shall be recompensed an hundredfold; and in the world to come, he shall give me eternal life."

And What Was the Outcome?

The enemy suffered an overwhelming defeat. God silenced the foe, and our Elector retained full liberty to use the Catechism in his country. Thus the Lord knows how to protect those who fear His Name, from the dangers that surround them.

The Heidelberg Catechism was introduced in The Netherlands at an early date, which was due especially to the efforts of Petrus Dathenus, the well known Court Chaplain of Frederick III, who labored so tirelessly for the cause of the Reformation in this region. The churches never have regretted accepting this Catechism. The many editions published gives evidence that the people of God derive much encouragement and comfort from this "book of comfort," and to this very day Catechism preaching is highly esteemed.

The Lord grant us to know that only comfort that matters both in life and death.

III. The Five Articles Against the Remonstrants or The Canons of Dort

We will now conclude with a word about the Five Articles Against the Remonstrants, commonly called the Canons of Dort.

It was to settle their dispute with the Remonstrants that the National Synod, held in Dordrecht in the years 1618-1619, composed these Articles.

The Remonstrants were the followers of Arminius, who was born in Oudewater in 1560. In 1588 he was a minister in Amsterdam, and made many statements in his preaching which were repugnant to the accepted truth. The doctrine of predestination being an offence to him, he ascribed to man a free will. Petrus Plancius opposed Arminius, and accused him of Pelagianism and Socinianism. Nevertheless, Arminius was appointed as Professor to Leiden in 1602. Objection to this appointment was made by the consistory of Amsterdam, and also by one Franciscus Gomarus, who was the only Professor of Theology in Leiden. But in a debate with Gomarus, the crafty Arminius so disguised his theses, that Gomarus retracted his objections; and the more so, because Arminius promised to adhere strictly to the principles expressed in the Confession and the Catechism. However, when he became Professor in 1603, he soon forgot his promise, and manifested what he really was. Gomarus opposed him in the full strength of the armor of biblical truth. A great disagreement arose among the students, and soon the whole church was brought in commotion.

The Arminians not only refused to leave the church, but used every cunning device to propagate their abominable doctrine among the people. Soon they demanded that the Confession of Faith become inoperative. But the opposition objected strenuously, and demanded that if any took exception to the approved standards of the church, he should openly and honestly make them known, leaving the decision thereof to the Synod. The Arminians, however, would not hear of this, knowing full well that they would lose their case before the Synod; therefore they sought the support of the civil authorities, whom they recognized as the lawful arbiters to settle any controversy in matters of faith. This was contrary to the Word of God. Although the authorities must defend the true church, they may not rule nor exercise any authority or dominion over the church. Many of the authorities in power at that time, however, were bitterly opposed in their hearts, yea, even antagonistic toward the strict Reformed doctrine. They were far more in agreement with Arminius, and besides, they felt greatly flattered by his current effort to augment their power. The rulers of Holland were especially susceptible to this flattery, and those of Utrecht were fully agreed.

John van Oldenbarneveldt, the Pension Commissioner of Holland, placed himself at the head of those opposing the Orthodox, who were now entering a very trying season. They were persecuted, and, in the name of tolerance, many faithful ministers were banished. Among many others, this also befell Rosaeus, minister at The Hague, who was the last remaining Reformed minister there. He was told to live in harmony and agreement with a certain Uytenbogaert, a fiery Remonstrant, and to partake of the Lord's Supper with him. For the sake of the truth, he refused, with the result that he was deposed. Oldenbarneveldt taunted him, "There you stand alone." But Rosaeus answered, "Not so sir! But God the Lord is with me, and as many thousands of truly pious as are yet remaining in this country." Thus the Lord strengthens His faithful servants in time of danger, and in days of scorn and reproach.

The Lord also altered the course of events. At the insistence of William Lodewijk, the pious governor of Vriesland, Prince Maurice became more resolute in his dealings. He caused the oath to be read to him, which he had sworn in 1586, and whereby he had solemnly pledged himself before God to defend the Reformed religion to the last drop of blood. Then he cried out, "I will protect this religion as long as I live." The conflict increased in violence. The States of Holland even recruited an army of their own, inciting thereby a civil war; but Maurice disbanded this home-militia. Oldenbarnevelt was taken captive, and, by a court of twenty-four judges, was sentenced to death. Finally a National Synod was called, to which assembly the Reformed theologians of other countries were also invited. The Synod was opened on November 13, 1618, and was in session until May of the following year.

At this Synod the Remonstrants were condemned; and the pure doctrine, founded on the Word of God, confirmed. Five Articles were drawn up, in which the five principal errors of the Remonstrants were rejected and condemned.

These Five Articles then, which contain the pure doctrine of God's Word, and are agreeable to the Confession of Faith, and were ratified by the National Synod of the Reformed Church held at Dordrecht in the year 1618-1619, are called the Canons of Dort. Furthermore, these Canons are divided into Five heads, the Third and Fourth Heads grouped as one; and consist of an aggregate of 59 Articles, and 34 Rejections of specific errors with which the church had for some time been troubled. The substance of which these various heads treat is as follows:

I. *Of Divine Predestination.*

II. *Of the Death of Christ, and Redemption of Men Thereby.*

III. and IV. *Of the Corruption of Man, his Conversion to God, and the manner Thereof.*

V. *Of the Perseverance of the Saints.*

Under each Head, and immediately after the doctrine has been explained, the errors appertaining thereto which Synod rejects and corrects are enumerated.

This concludes our short historical summary of the Three Forms of Unity. That it may serve to convince us of the great value of our Doctrinal Standards. It was under His Providential guidance that the Lord caused them to be born in the violent struggle of His church; and although they by no means are to be placed on an equal plane with God's Word, yet they are founded on Scripture, and are more than mere human documents. May the Lord build His church thereon and keep us faithful to the doctrines confessed therein.

The Compendium

This work is an abridgment of the Heidelberg Catechism, compiled by Herman Faukeel, minister at Middelburg, and published in 1611. It was later recommended by the Synod of Dordrecht.

It is evident from the contents that the Compendium is an extraction of the Heidelberg Catechism. They are both divided into three parts, viz., Misery, Deliverance and Thankfulness, as follows:

The Catechism:

  I. *Of the Misery of Man,* Lord's Day 1 to 4.

  II. *Of Man's Deliverance,* Lord's Day 5 to 31.

  III. *Of Thankfulness,* Lord's Day 32 to 52.

The Compendium.

  I. *Of the Misery of Man,* Questions 1 to 13.

  II. *Of Man's Deliverance,* Questions 14 to 63.

  III. *Of Thankfulness,* Questions 64 to 74.

The section on Thankfulness is, in proportion, much shorter in the Compendium than in the Catechism. The reason for this is, that the questions dealing with the Ten Commandments are omitted in the first, whereas they supply material for 11 Lord's Days in the Catechism.

*   *   *

PART I

Of the Misery of Man

QUESTIONS 1-7

The Compendium corresponds with the Heidelberg Catechism, as is already seen in the very first question, which is a repetition of the second question of Lord's Day I, that reads thus:

Qu. 1: *How many things are necessary for thee to know, that thou enjoying real comfort, mayest live and die happily?*

An important question, indeed!

This life is full of anxiety: days of trouble and distress: of sorrow and mourning. Moses says in Ps. 90, "The strength of our days is labor and sorrow." And so it is, because we have subjected ourselves to God's judgments; and for the sake of our sins, the ground is cursed. Moreover, it is appointed unto men once to die, but after this the judgment. How fearful to us should be thoughts of death and of being summoned before God's tribunal.

But now there is a comfort that surpasses and removes the grief and sorrow in this life, and takes away the fear of death. Should we then not seek this only comfort to obtain true happiness?

But this comfort is wrought by the Lord alone in the way which is shown by the answer. This answer teaches us how many things are necessary, viz., "Three: first, how great my sins and miseries are; the second, how I may be delivered from all my sins and miseries; the third, how I shall express my gratitude to God for such deliverance.' '

Misery, deliverance and gratitude are thus the three things which must be known, that we, enjoying real comfort, may live and die happily. This knowledge is more than a mere knowing that we are miserable, that there is deliverance in Christ, and that it behooves us to honor Him with our gratitude. We all know this well enough out of Scripture. The Lord says emphatically

13

in Jer. 3:13, "Only acknowledge thine iniquity, that thou hast transgressed against the Lord thy God." And the Apostle declares in Rom. 3:9, 10, "For we have before proved both Jews and Gentiles, that they are all under sin; as it is written, There is none righteous, no, not one."

The deliverance in Christ is spoken of in practically every page of God's Word. "For the Son of man is come to seek and to save that which was lost," Luke 19:10. And that this deliverance obliges to gratitude, is shown in Ps. 116:17, where it is written, "I will offer to thee the sacrifice of thanksgiving, and will call upon the name of the Lord"; and in Ps. 50:14, "Offer unto God thanksgiving, and pay thy vows unto the Most High."

But although we all may know that these three things are mentioned in God's Word, nevertheless this is not a *knowing* of them to our only comfort and happiness. The knowledge of which the instructor speaks, is the fruit of spiritual illumination in the heart of the elect. He opens the blind eyes, and causes the state of misery to be known. O, then such an one finds himself to be in a totally lost state; then all rest is denied him, that he may obtain deliverance in Christ through faith, and the Lord may be honored in him through His own work.

And be especially mindful of this, that experimental knowledge is indispensable in order to enjoy real comfort and live and die happily. There are many who do not want to hear of *this* knowledge. They glory in a Jesus of whom they have heard and read, but who never has been revealed in them. Their sin and misery has never been discovered unto them. They quickly pass over that first thing which is necessary for them to know, viz., their misery. But then what need have they of Jesus? Their praise and glory of God is lip worship, and a stench in the nostrils of the Almighty. The Lord keep us from self-deceit, and open our blind eyes to acquaint us with our deplorable state of misery. Therefore He impresses the holy demand of His perfect law upon the souls of His people. To this our thoughts are directed in:

Qu. 2:   *Whence knowest thou thy misery?*

Answer: Out of the law of God.

The Compendium now begins treating of the misery of man, in such a manner, that it deals:

first, Of the state of our misery, (Questions 2 to 7),

second, Of the origin of our misery, (Questions 8 to 13)

In the Holland language the equivalent of the word miserable means foreign or far away; to be an outcast. Thus Absalom, after murdering Amnon, lived in banishment in Gesur, removed from his fatherland, and without seeing the face of his father David. The state of misery of us all is, that because of sin, we are banished out of fellowship with God and are driven out of paradise.

First of all then, we must consider *the state* of our misery, which is spoken of in this lesson, and with which we become acquainted out of the law of God, through the discovering work of the Spirit. The laws which the Lord gave upon Sinai were of three kinds, viz.:

1. The CEREMONIAL laws;
2. The CIVIL laws;
3. The MORAL law, or TEN COMMANDMENTS.

The ceremonial laws were the laws of Israel's religion. They speak of:

a. SACRED PERSONS: The Priests and Levites;
b. SACRED PLACES: The Court, the Holy Place (or Sanctuary), and the Most Holy;
c. SACRED SEASONS: The Passover, Pentecost and the Feast of Tabernacles;
d. SACRED THINGS: Sacrifices.

The ceremonial laws are not applicable in the Church of the New Testament; they are fulfilled in Christ. There no longer are priests after the order of Aaron; we no longer go to the earthly sanctuary at Jerusalem, nor observe the feasts of the Old Testament, nor bring sacrifices of beasts. That all has been done away with. The Lord Himself made an end of the ceremonial laws when He rent the veil in twain from the top to the bottom. Thus old age did not cause the veil to be rent; for a hanging curtain that tears of age, tears crosswise; but the veil of the temple was rent from the top. Yes, rent in twain by God. Therewith the Lord declared that the service of types and shadows was ended.

None might ever look into the Most Holy Place. When the High Priest entered therein once a year, he was obliged to close the veil behind him; then no priest was permitted to tarry in the sanctuary. So strict was God's injunction, that none should cast even one glance into the Holy of Holies. But when Christ died upon Golgotha, and brought the only sacrifice that appeased God's wrath, and restored His Church into His fellowship, then God rent the veil. The earthly sanctuary was done away with; the types and shadows are fulfilled in Christ. The Church of the New Covenant has a High Priest, it is true; One, however, Who is greater than Aaron; Who is entered, not into the ceremonial earthly sanctuary, but into the heavenly sanctuary, sitting on the right hand of the Majesty of God. The ceremonial feast days are replaced by the spiritual joy which gives to the elect joy in God; and in place of sacrifices of bulls and goats, that could not take away sin, Christ is given to the Church of God, Who with one offering in eternity, hath perfected forever them that are sanctified.

The ceremonial laws have been done away with.

The Civil laws of Israel, are likewise no longer in effect for any nation.

Those Civil laws concerned the civil and political life of Israel. That people was a theocracy, i.e., it was governed by the immediate direction of God. Israel therefore received its laws directly from God. The Lord Himself acquainted the people with them through Moses. No civil authorities nor representatives of the people deliberated over the law for the nation's government. The Lord was Israel's judge, lawgiver and king, Isaiah 33:22. No people can receive better laws than Israel had. And the question arises whether it would be proper for us to discard all the manmade laws, under which many of us so often sigh, and replace them with the God-given laws. No, indeed, that cannot be; for, after all, those civil laws of Israel were appointed for the theocratic people, and become void with *all* ceremonial types. The counterpart of Israel is not a political nation, but it is the Church of the New Covenant. In that Church Christ reigns as King, and none but His laws are in effect. But His Kingdom is not of this world. Therefore when Jesus had finished His work upon earth, Jerusalem was destroyed and Israel ceased to exist as a nation. And although the wishes of many should be realized to gather all the Jews in Palestine; yea, though they should discover a lineal descendant of David, and make him king, even then Israel shall never, never again become what it formerly was; it shall nevermore become a theocratic nation. O, that they would learn to bend the knee for King Jesus, Whom they reject from age to age, and Whose blood they have brought upon themselves, and through obduracy continue to do. Therein lies the profound cause of the Jews' terrible misery. O, that *we* then, considering God's judgment over Israel, might come to understand the words of Ps. 2:12, "Kiss the Son, lest he be angry, and ye perish from the way, when his wrath is kindled but a little."

The ceremonial and civil laws of Israel have thus been done away with, although there is in them a moral standard which is applicable for all ages. But as they were given to Israel, the people of types and shadows, they are now void.

The Moral law, or Ten Commandments, however, is not abrogated. This law is everlasting. The distinction between this law and the other two kinds of laws first mentioned, already became evident in the giving of the law itself. For the Ten Commandments were written in two tables of stone; not the ceremonial and civil laws. Whatever is written in stone, endures. In the present day, small tables of stone are discovered, which are three thousand or more years old, and are still legible; and likewise think of the many ancient tombstones. Whatever is written in stone, endures. Thus the Lord manifested the everlasting character of the Ten Commandments when He gave these upon two tables of stone. These Ten Commandments did have a ceremonial significance attached to them which concerned only Israel, as, for instance, the sanctifying of the seventh day; but the moral law is not abolished. It comprises the rule of God's will for all peoples for all ages. Therefore that law was definitely not for the Jews alone. The Lord Jesus said, "Think not that I am come to destroy the law, or the prophets: I am not come to destroy, but to fulfill."

This law was engraved by God on the heart of Adam. He proclaimed the Ten Commandments from Mt. Sinai, where He established a covenant with His people. This covenant was not merely an outward covenant with only temporal promises of the earthly Canaan and of rich earthly blessings! Indeed not! This covenant was . . . THE COVENANT OF GRACE!

In it eternal salvation was bequeathed unto God's elect in Christ, even though this covenant was revealed in a national form.

We must distinguish the form of revelation from the essence of the covenant.

The Covenant of Grace is an essential covenant made between two parties. These parties cannot be the Father and the Son as the First and the Second Person in the Divine Essence. In the Essence of God there are no parties.

The parties of this Covenant are God the Father, acting for the Divine Persons, and Christ, as Head of the elect. The question is hereby also answered, whether the Spirit had part in the making of this covenant; for the Spirit as well as the Son acted in the Person of the Father. According to the economy of the Divine Persons, the Father maintained the injured justice, and required of Christ, Who represented the elect, perfect satisfaction, and promised Him the heathen for His inheritance, and the uttermost parts of the earth for His possession. Christ has taken upon Himself to perform all the conditions of the covenant, since the elect were unable to perform a single one of these conditions. And by virtue of this holy covenant-transaction, the elect are given unto Christ for His possession, as the Lord Jesus said, "Father, thine they were, and Thou gavest them me," John 17:6. The Covenant of Grace is established in Christ with the elect from eternity, and, in time, they are received effectually into the covenant. Of this Covenant, Christ is the Head, as all our Reformed theologians have always testified. They, who deny that Christ is the Head of the Covenant of Grace, banish the precious works of our old writers out of the home and church. Thus have they cleared the way for their new doctrines. The Lord keep us from ever inclining toward such a covenant-enervating doctrine.

To this one Covenant of Grace, however, the Lord has given several forms of revelation:

The PARTICULAR form,   (Adam....to....Abraham);
The PATRIARCHAL form,   (Abraham....to....Moses);
The NATIONAL form,   (Moses....to....Christ);
The ECCLESIASTICAL form, (under the New Testament).

Many who do not essentially belong to the Covenant of Grace, nevertheless do stand in an external relation to the covenant. For they are not all Israel, which are of Israel. They are not all true covenant children who are baptized and make confession. Yet they live within the confines of the revelation of the covenant. As to the form of the covenant, it was national in the establishing thereof at Mt. Sinai, but the essence of the covenant was the Covenant of Grace, that bequeathes salvation in Christ to the elect, and to them alone. Likewise, the law was also given under the blood of the covenant, i.e., the blood of Christ. Otherwise the people would have been consumed under the curse of the law.

Now the knowledge of sin is by the law. So says God's Word, in Rom 3:20, "By the law is the knowledge of sin." This knowledge is therefore not by faith. The law declares man guilty and condemnable before God. It condemns every one that continueth not in all things which are written in the book of the law to do them. In the efficacious, irresistible conviction of the Spirit, it prostrates the sinner before God as one deserving of eternal death. Faith, however, causes the soul to mount in Christ out of the depth of misery to complete deliverance.

Have we already learned to know the strength of God's law after this manner? It is indispensable for us all to learn to flee to Christ in truth.

Now we come to the next question.

Qu. 4: *How are the Ten Commandments divided?*

Answer: Into two tables.

As taught in the fifth and sixth questions, the first table of the law contains four commandments, and the second contains six.

Rome considers the first table of the law to contain but three commandments. They combine the first and second commandment, thereby deleting the second commandment out of the law; and then, in order to arrive at the prescribed number of commandments in the moral law, they divide the tenth into two commandments.

If there is anything at all that testifies against Romish image worship, then it is this deforming of God's law. The second commandment prohibits the worship of images, with which Rome is filled; and, in order to preserve this awful, idolatrous image worship, they mutilate even the law of God. There certainly is a considerable distinction between the first and second commandments. The first commandment teaches us *Whom* we shall serve, viz., God only, and not idols. The second commandment, however, prescribes the manner in which the Lord will be served; and that is not by means of images.

Moreover, how does Rome disentangle itself by dividing the tenth commandment; for what then is the ninth, and what the tenth commandment? The clauses of the tenth commandment in Exodus 20 follow an order different from that used in Deuteronomy 5. In Ex. 20 it is stated, "Thou shalt not covet thy neighbour's house, thou shalt not covet thy neighbour's wife," but in Deut. 5. the wife is mentioned first, and then the house. Now if Rome says, "The ninth commandment is: Thou shalt not covet thy neighbor's house," it is in conflict with Deut. 5; and if they claim that the ninth commandment reads, "Neither shalt thou desire thy neighbour's wife," then Ex. 20 witnesses against them. O, that blind, idolatrous Rome!

Not three, but four commandments are contained in the first table; and six in the second.

Qu. 5:   *Which is the sum of what God requires of thee in the four commandments of the first table?*

Answer: That I love the Lord my God, with all my heart, with all my soul, with all my mind, and with all my strength: this is the first and great commandment. (Matt. 22:37, 38)

With these words the Lord Jesus tells us that God is to be loved with all our faculties, both will and understanding. This love toward God does not consist in words and a slavish, legal bondage; true love does not hold the heart far from God, but causes one to esteem Him above all else in the world, with all that is within us, Ps. 103:1. This is what God requires in His law. It is the first and great commandment, because the obedience to all other commandments flows from this.

The second table requires love to our neighbor, as is taught in the sixth question.

Qu. 6: *Which is the sum of what God commands thee in the six commandments of the second table?*

Answer: That I love my neighbor as myself; on these two commandments hang the whole law and the prophets. (Matt. 22:39, 40).

The Lord Jesus expresses plainly who our neighbor is in the parable of the good Samaritan. In Luke 10 we are told of a certain lawyer who asked the Lord, "What shall I do to inherit eternal life?"

It was not out of a holy anxiety that this was asked by the lawyer, but to tempt Jesus.

Then it was that Christ directed him to the observance of the law. In an effort to hide his embarrassment, the lawyer asked, "And who is my neighbor?" Jesus then spoke the parable of the good Samaritan, which parable we surely all know. Actually the Lord answered this lawyer with a counter-question: Just ask that unfortunate man, who fell among the thieves, who his neighbor is. Shall he say: that priest, that Levite, who passed him by without any feeling of compassion? Surely not! But he shall answer: "The Samaritan, although an enemy of Israel, he is my neighbor." Now the Lord says: Do thou likewise. Even your enemy must feel constrained to say of you: He is my neighbor. All mankind is to be considered as our neighbor; God hath made of one blood all nations of men, Acts 17:26. God requires charity to all mankind, even to our enemies. He requires of us to love them as ourselves: i.e., entirely; with a perfect mind; seeking their welfare, as Paul incites the saints at Rome: "Be kindly affectioned one to another with brotherly love; in honor preferring one another; Romans 12:10; and in chapter 13:10, the Apostle writes, "Love worketh no ill to his neighbor."

And this commandment is no smaller nor of less importance than the first commandment; it is explicitly stated: The second is like unto it. Also, the Lord did not say: The first and greatest commandment; but the great. The second is also great, like unto the first. God's requirement written on the second table of the law is not less than that expressed in the first table.

O, let us not undervalue any of God's commandments. Whosoever offendeth in one point, is guilty of all. God's justice requires perfect obedience to all commandments, and that demand is stated in one word: LOVE; perfect love toward God and toward our neighbor, for love is the fulfilling of the law, Rom. 13:10. But that is exactly why it is impossible for man in the state of nature to keep the law.

Qu. 7: *Canst thou keep all these things perfectly?*

Answer: In no wise: for I am prone by nature to hate God and my neighbor: and to transgress the commandments of God in thought, word and deed.

Indeed, is that truly so? Is it really so bad with natural man, that he not only hates God, but also his neighbor? We surely love our parents, brothers, sisters and children? Even they who forsake God's Word, and turn their backs upon His service, still have a natural affection toward their neighbor. How then can the instructor say: I am prone by nature to hate God and my neighbor? And this expression definitely does not mean: I am somewhat inclined to this hate; but by 'prone' is meant, that the principle of our existence is hatred; we are hateful and hating one another in the root of our heart, by virtue of our fall in Adam. We did not bring any love along out of Paradise, but hatred. And a natural affection is not a consequence of our fall, but is of common grace which God shows unto all mankind in order that the world might be borne by Him until the very last of the elect shall have been gathered in. The answer of the Compendium is in accordance with God's Word. Because the carnal mind is enmity against God: for it is not subject to the law of God, neither indeed can be, Rom. 8:7. We are haters of God, Rom. 1:30; hateful and hating one another, Titus 3:3.

Therefore it is also absolutely impossible to keep the law; that requires love. Though we do all that is written in the law: and though we become like unto the rich young man, yet there would be in all our doings nothing but a transgression of God's law. We give hatred for love. Whatever man *can* do: precept upon precept: line upon line: he cannot love what he hates. We are transgressors of God's law in thought, word and deed. Man by nature shall never be able to keep a single one of God's commandments, even for a moment. Alas! how appalling is the state in which we all are by nature. We increase our guilt; heap sin upon sin, to the coming of the great day of judgment; except we find reconciliation in Him, Who has satisfied the law perfectly by His active and passive obedience.

Dear students, may it please the Lord to discover us by His holy law; that we trust not in our own righteousnesses, for they are as filthy rags. But that Christ may clothe us with His righteousness, which only is acceptable to God.

That the law, to that end, may become unto us a schoolmaster to bring us unto Christ.

PART II

Of the Origin of Our Misery
QUESTIONS 8-13

In the first seven questions of the First Part of The Compendium, the misery was indicated in which all mankind is by nature; that we are prone to hate God and our neighbor, instead of loving them. Consequently we are transgressors of God's commandments, and can keep none of them at all.

Now the instructor is to show whence this depravity proceeds. He asks:

Qu. 8: *Hath God created thee naturally so wicked and perverse?*

Answer: By no means: but He created me good and after His own image, in the true knowledge of God, in righteousness and in holiness.

The cause of our misery therefore lies not in God's creation. If it did, it would be God's fault that we are so wretched. But this is not so, for God has created us good and after His own image. God can create nothing but that which is perfect. Therefore Scripture states explicitly, "God saw every thing that He had made, and, behold, it was very good." That applied particularly to the creation of man.

Was then the creation of man perfect?

Indeed; if not, a defect could be charged in that which God had wrought, and that cannot be. Although man, created in perfection, could attain to greater heights, it by no means implies any imperfection. Moreover, God created man after His own image and likeness, which description was never given even unto angels. Man was the gem of God's creation. Paul writes in Heb. 1:3, that the Son of God, who is true and eternal God, and not created or made, is the 'express image' of God's person. But this is not so of man, for Adam was created in the 'likeness' of God's image.

This image consisted in knowledge, righteousness and holiness. See Eph. 4:24, and Col. 3:10, where Paul teaches that the regeneration of the elect is after the image of Him who created man. And this regeneration is in knowledge (Col. 3:10) and righteousness and holiness (Eph. 4:24). Such was also the creation of man.

Adam knew God, the One and Triune God, and so did Eve. It was the source of their soul-satisfying happiness. They also had knowledge of good and evil, and a conception of the punishment which God had threatened, as is plainly shown by Eve's answer to the serpent. And how did Adam's knowledge shine forth in the naming of every living creature according to its nature!

This image consisted further in righteousness and holiness. Thus man lived in immediate communion, and in the friendship of God. O, in what a glorious state was man created!

Therefore the teaching of Pelagius that man was created neither good nor evil, is abominable. This heretic taught:

1. That man was a 'tabula rasa'; i.e., a blank tablet, upon which nothing was written, neither good nor bad, and that all habits of vice and virtue are acquired through practice and imitation.

2. That the image of God consisted merely in natural faculties of the soul; in the outward posture of the body, and in dominion over the animal kingdom.

3. That Adam was created mortal, with death therefore a natural consequence, and not a result of sin.

In order to refute the erroneous doctrines of the Pelagians and their spiritual seed, the Remonstrants, it is imperative for us to see aright that God's image here spoken of belonged essentially to man's being, and is not something merely added to it. Furthermore, man was not created 'in' God's image, as some Neo-Kohlbruggians teach, but 'after' God's image. In a word: this image was part of man's essential being. When man lost God's image, his very being was impaired.

We can consider the image of God in:

(a)   a restricted sense; and,

(b)   a wider sense.

In a restricted sense it consists in knowledge, righteousness and holiness, which were imprinted on the soul. In the fall, therefore, we lost the image of God in its entirety; man did not become sick or diseased, but fell dead!

In a wider sense the whole of man was created after God's image, as manifested by his entire appearance: his dominion over the creatures; and the immortality of his soul. Our Confession of Faith refers to this, (Art. 14), speaking of a few remains of God's image which man has retained. Included in these few remains is man's inborn knowledge. This innate knowledge is an inherent consciousness of a higher Being, whom we call God, (Art. 1). Every person is born with this consciousness. Atheists are not born, but made, and they speak against their conscience. In the fall, man became neither devil nor beast, but remained a rational, moral creature, endowed with understanding and will, although totally depraved.

Thus we see that man is:

(a)   created perfect and good, and not a 'tabula rasa', i.e., a blank tablet;

(b)   God's image consisted in knowledge, righteousness and holiness, and not in outward things;

(c)   with God's image man was immortal. Death is not a natural consequence, but is the wages of sin, Rom. 6:23;

(d)   God's image was part of man's very being.

Man's misery and his wretched state are therefore no fault of God's creation. We read in Eccl. 7:29, "Lo, this only have I found, that God hath made man upright."

Qu.   9:   *Whence then proceeds that depravity which is in thee?*

Answer: From the fall and disobedience of Adam and Eve in Paradise; hence our nature is become so corrupt, that we are all conceived and born in sin.

The origin of our misery lies therefore in the fall and disobedience of Adam and Eve, and not in God's creation. God created man in such a manner, that, although he could attain to greater heights, he also could transgress and fall. Not that God had any part at all in the actual fall of man, but in His incomprehensible counsel and will God left room for sin to reveal itself, so that, by this abomination, He would be everlastingly glorified, in righteousness as well as in mercy. The fall of man was decreed by God. Man's forsaking his Creator did not suddenly overtake God, for He knew it from eternity. God knew it because He had decreed it, and in the knowledge that His decrees would be executed.

Was the fall of man then *inevitable?*

Yes, it was, in respect to God's immutable decree; and No, it was not inevitable, in respect to the faculties with which he was endowed to remain standing.

Here we must distinguish a two-fold necessity:

1. A necessity of consequence, out of the foregoing or previous decree;
2. An actual or immediate necessity, whereby something must be accomplished by reason of God's decree, without the concurrence of the creature.

This last concerns the inanimate and irrational creation. The sun rises and sets, and water must of necessity flow down hill, etc., without these creatures concurring therein. The same applies to the plant and animal creation, who bear fruit and act further as God has decreed, although these creatures do not concur therein knowingly or intentionally; they act, as it were, unconsciously. Here is an actual or immediate necessity, so that is accomplished, what God has decreed.

With rational creatures, however, there is a voluntary acting, whereof the primary cause is God's decree, and the secondary cause the acting creature. This creature acts voluntarily; the secret decree does in no wise coerce him. Therefore God's decree is not the rule of the rational creature's actions; but this rule is God's law. According to this law, the actions of man are adjudged good or evil. However, neither the sovereignty nor the necessity of God's decree do at all remove the rational creature's freedom or responsibility.

Thus man (as did the angels) fell voluntarily, and wilfully, carrying the full responsibility of his act.

A few examples may make this clear:

Esau was an outcast, a reprobate, who was not to obtain salvation; but the birthright was his, and to this birthright the promise of the Messiah was attached. But what did Esau do? He despised his birthright. He was a mocker and profane, and sold his birthright for a mess of pottage. Who was at fault here? Could Esau rightfully find fault with his Creator? Esau wrought his own destruction, as God had decreed from eternity.

We have another example in Pharaoh. The Lord told Moses that he would harden Pharaoh's heart, that He might be honored upon him. But Pharaoh contrived his own downfall, when he steadfastly refused to obey the word of the Lord. "Who is the Lord," said he, "that I should obey him?" So Pharaoh brought about his own destruction, although God had previously decreed it.

And a third one is Judas the traitor. The Psalms prophesy what God had decreed in eternity concerning him. Judas necessarily had to be, to betray Christ. He nevertheless acted wilfully, and then cried out in despair: "I have done it; I have betrayed innocent blood."

Thus the counsel of God is performed by every creature, and none make a move independent of this counsel, whether good or evil; yet, what he does, he is accountable for.

And so it was with the fall of man. Although decreed by God, Adam and Eve must bear the responsibility thereof, because they wilfully forsook God.

The angels that fell were the first of God's creation that sinned; they became devils. Then man rebelled against his Maker, committing the transgression of disobedience voluntarily and wilfully. In the fall of Adam and Eve, the human nature became so depraved, that all mankind is conceived and born in sin.

Qu. 10: *What was that disobedience?*

Answer: That they did eat of the fruit of the tree, which God had forbidden them.

This tree was the tree of knowledge of good and evil, and man was not permitted to eat thereof.

Was this transgression so great then, that, for the mere eating of the fruit of this forbidden tree, Adam and Eve and all their posterity should be punished with eternal death? Was not this punishment too severe?

IN NO WISE; for,

1. Man knew that God had forbidden the eating thereof;
2. This tree was the tree of God's authority;
3. In the eating of this tree, man made God a liar;
4. By his eating of this tree, man severed himself from God.

1. Man knew that God had forbidden the eating thereof.

Neither Adam nor Eve could plead ignorance in the committing of this sin. This is shown by Eve at the time Satan accosted her with his subtle temptation, by means of a serpent, (which was a real serpent, created by God) when she answered that they might eat of every tree except the tree of the knowledge of good and evil.

2. This tree was the tree of God's authority.

God alone knew what was good, and what was not good for His creatures; man had only to obey His command: to do what God had commanded, and abstain from that which God had forbidden.

To this Satan alluded when he said, "Ye shall be as gods, knowing good and evil." Not inferring thereby that, as they now knew only the good, they would likewise know evil if they ate of this tree. Not at all; something more subtle lay in Satan's words; for what was desirable for man in attaining to the knowledge of evil? The knowledge of good and evil belonged to the "being as gods. Satan suggested to man that he could free himself from God's authority; make himself Lord and Master, loosed from God, and being judge of good and evil. Therefore Adam and Eve assaulted God's supreme authority by eating of the fruit of the tree of the knowledge of good and evil. It is immaterial what kind of fruit was found on this tree, but this we know, that God had forbidden the eating thereof, and also that man was obliged to respect God's commandment and submit himself to his Creator. This transgression was therefore so heinous, in that it was rebellion against God.

3. In the eating thereof man made God a liar.

God said, "In the day that thou eatest thereof, thou shalt surely die," and Satan said, "Ye shall not surely die." One of these two statements was a falsehood. And, behold, man believed the saying of Satan, and made God a liar.

Is this then a small transgression?

4. By his eating of this tree, man severed himself from God.

We have already shown that by the deceitful assertion, "Ye shall be as gods, knowing good and evil," Satan insinuated that man could free himself from God's authority, and make himself Lord and Master. How then could this transgression be equitably punished by any means other than death? No, indeed, the punishment is not too severe, for outside of God there is no life, and whosoever disjoins himself from God must die.

So we see that Adam and Eve's punishment was righteous, and suitable to their transgression; but how are we involved therein?

Qu. 11: *Does the disobedience of Adam concern us?*

Answer: Certainly; for he is the father of us all; and we have all sinned in him.

Why is reference here made only to the sin of Adam, and not to that of Eve? Was not she the mother of us all, as Adam was the father of us all?

The reason for this is that the imputation of sin is considered in the covenant-relation, and not in our natural relation. God established the Covenant of Works with Adam, and in *him* with all his descendants.

Adam was not *created* in the Covenant of Works; for then there would have been no actual covenant-making, and consequently no covenant-breaking. But in His condescending mercy the Lord made a covenant with Adam at the time of creation; and he with God. Adam made this covenant with God voluntarily.

Could Adam then have refused to make this covenant?

Although Adam was a free agent in regard to his entering into this covenant, yet it was impossible for him to decline, for it was his greatest delight and joy to please God. Thus we see that Adam entered into this Covenant of Works with God of his own free will; not constrainedly, but willingly and gladly. As the federal head, Adam represented all his posterity in the Covenant of Works; they stood in him, and likewise, they fell in him.

The two parties concluding this covenant were therefore God and Adam, with Adam representing all mankind. He is consequently called the head of the Covenant of Works. The head of the covenant is he who represents those who are included in the covenant, and it is therefore not God, but Adam who is the head of the Covenant of Works, and Christ (representing the elect) Who is the head of the Covenant of Grace; not God the Father.

In the Covenant of Works, God promised life eternal upon an obedient performance. This is the special promise of the covenant, which, in regard to the doctrines of the Pelagians, Socinians and Remonstrants, we must definitely insist upon. They deny the existence of the Covenant of Works, and consequently also the fall of man. Pelagius maintains that Adam's fall does not affect his posterity; that sin is by imitation only; and that man still has a free will, able to do good as well as evil.

We must never lose sight of that!

The promise of life eternal and the beatific vision of undisturbed, uninterrupted communion with God, flows not from that inborn, innate law in Adam's heart which God had placed there in creation, but was the special promise of the covenant. If Adam had complied with the conditions of the covenant, then he, and in him all his descendants, would have obtained everlasting life. By his transgression Adam plunged himself and all mankind into everlasting destruction.

Although no specific mention is made in Gen. 2 of the Covenant of Works; or in Gen. 3:15 of the Covenant of Grace, still parts of the covenants are there described. We further read of the breach of this Covenant of Works in Hosea 6:7; and throughout the entire Scriptures eternal life is made dependent upon obedience to the law; see Lev. 18:5, and Matt. 19:17. Paul also speaks repeatedly of that obedience which is of the law, Romans 3:27; 10:5; Gal. 4:24. All this confirms the statement that everlasting life was once promised upon the performance of the law. This was not by virtue of creation, but through the establishing of the Covenant of Works by God.

Thus we stand in a two-fold relation to Adam:

a. In a natural relation, because he is the father of us all;

b. In a covenant-relation, because he was the head of the Covenant of Works, and therein represented all his posterity.

Adam could properly represent all his descendants in the Covenant of Works, because they were all in him.

As the imputation of sin is not out of the natural relation, Israel's complaint in Jer. 31.29, is not at all appropriate, "The fathers have eaten a sour grape, and the children's teeth are set on edge." The people wanted to put the blame upon their fathers, but the Lord answered, "Every one shall die for his own iniquity; every man that eateth the sour grape, his teeth shall be set on edge," Jer. 31:30. The children are not being punished merely for the sins of their natural fathers; neither is the sin of Adam imputed unto his descendants because he is the father of us all, but because he was our covenant-head. Imputation is not out of the natural relation, but out of the covenant-relation. It is likewise out of the covenant-relation that the righteousness of Christ is imputed unto the elect. Adam was the head of the Covenant of Works; Christ is the Head of the Covenant of Grace.

Whereas the imputation of guilt is out of the covenant-relation, and not the natural, therefore it is Adam's transgression which is imputed unto his posterity, and not the sin of Eve. This is verified by the Apostle in Rom. 5:12-19, where it is mentioned and repeated five times, that by one man, (not two people) sin entered into the world: i.e., by Adam. And however many sins our forefather Adam may have committed in his long life, only one offence is imputed unto us, as is explained once and again in Rom. 5:12-19; one offence, namely, that of Adam's covenant breach.

It was thus one offence, committed by one man! The transgression of the covenant-head imputed unto us out of the covenant-relation! That sin of disobedience by Adam concerns us all, and makes all his descendants guilty of eternal death.

One question more:

Did not God lay a snare for man? You may say, "Alas! Why was there ever a forbidden tree in Paradise! Why did God ever permit Satan to speak by means of the serpent! Man could have remained forever in the state of bliss he enjoyed in Paradise."

No, indeed, God did not spread a snare to entangle his creature. He had endowed man with understanding and will, in distinction from the irrational and inanimate creation. And how would the glory of man's creation have been fully revealed? Only if he had shown that his serving of God was the very desire of his soul, and not because he had no choice. The sun and moon, animals and plants obey the ordinances which God has established, and, while in creation God impressed the moral law upon the heart of man, and made entire conformity to it his indispensable duty, yet, to test whether rational man obeyed God above all these creatures, the Lord God was pleased to give man a positive law, restricting him from the use of the fruit of a particular tree of the garden.

God summed up the duty of man in this single positive injunction, and constituted his abstaining from the fruit of this tree the test of his obedience to the divine authority. Thence the probation; thence the use of the serpent.

And, behold, here Adam and Eve (and we in him) did knowingly and willingly leave the path which led to life everlasting, and to a full display of God's glorious creation, to our eternal destruction. God did not ensnare man, but man plunged himself into death: spiritual, temporal and eternal death.

Yes, at that time spiritual death entered, as we see in the next question.

Qu. 12: *Are we then incapable of doing any good of ourselves, and prone to all manner of wickedness?*

Answer: Indeed we are: unless we are regenerated by the Spirit of God.

This is the spiritual death in which all mankind, because of their covenant relation to Adam, is born. None is capable of performing anything spiritually good; and our best performances are as filthy rags. Therefore, any who rely upon their good works, shall be found wanting. We must become regenerated, as the Lord Jesus said to Nicodemus, (John 3:3), "Verily, verily, I say unto thee, Except a man be born again, he cannot see the kingdom of God."

What is regeneration?

In our "Canons of Dort", under the Third and Fourth Heads of Doctrine, Art. 12, we read, "And this is the regeneration so highly celebrated in Scripture, and denominated a new creation: a resurrection from the dead, a making alive, which God works in us without our aid."

It takes place, therefore, when the Lord quickens the creature. We are either regenerated, or unregenerated; either living or dead. We cannot be both, but are definitely the one or the other. In our unregenerate state we are prone to all manner of wickedness; and if we break not forth in all manner of wickedness, it is only because of God's restraining hand.

Alas! That is the state of profound misery we are in by nature, because of our fall in Adam. For the fall was not a blessed thing, as some suppose, but indeed a very wretched and calamitous event: God's attributes were injured; man subjected himself to the righteous judgment of God; and, because of the fall, the very ground was accursed.

Qu. 13: *Will God suffer such disobedience and corruption to go unpunished?*

Answer: By no means: but in his just judgment will punish them, both in time and eternity, as it is written: "Cursed is every one that continueth not in all things, which are written in the book of the law, to do them." Gal. 3:10.

So abominable and dreadful is sin, that, if God did not punish the same, He would cease to be God. This punishment is both temporal and eternal. All the misery that is in the world is the effect of sin, and will be followed at death with eternal punishment in everlasting fire, first according to the soul, and then according to both body and soul.

Dear students, may the Lord open our eyes to see the state of misery we are in by nature, and give us to realize our dreadful fall in Adam, that we may obtain redemption in Christ by faith.

PART III

Of the Mediator

QUESTIONS 14-18

Whereas the misery of man is treated in Part I, which covers the first thirteen questions, The Compendium commences with the next question to speak, in Part II, of man's deliverance, (Questions 14-63).

First of all we are directed to the Mediator, by Whom only deliverance out of our state of misery is possible.

Qu. 14: *By what means canst thou escape this punishment, and be again received into favor?*

Answer: By such a Mediator, who is in one person very God, and a real, righteous man.

Deliverance out of the state of our misery is not possible, unless perfect satisfaction is made to the justice of God. To accomplish this, a Mediator is needed. A Mediator is one who interposes between two parties, to reconcile them. In order that the guilty sinner may escape the well-deserved punishment and be again received into favor, a Mediator is requisite to stand betwixt a God Who is wroth because of sin, and the guilty sinner who has not a single farthing with which to pay. A Mediator is needed Who takes away the punishment by a perfect satisfaction, and restores to fellowship with God. By "being again received into favor," is meant however, restoring again to God's favor and fellowship.

This Mediator must be very God, and a real, righteous man. The requirement that he be very man comprises:

1. That he have soul and body;
2. That he belong to our human race.

Righteous man means: to be without sin.

And why must this Mediator be:

A. Very God?
B. Very man?
C. Righteous man?

A. The Mediator must be very God.
1. To support the assumed human nature in the bearing of God's fierce wrath to the end·
2. To give an infinite value to His mediatorial sacrifice.

1. No mere creature can bear the burden of God's everlasting wrath, and deliver others therefrom. Although one had come without sin, he would have perished under the burden of God's wrath, and been unable to bear it to the end. Verily, Christ would have succumbed in the Garden of Gethsemane, when His sweat was as it were great drops of blood falling down to the ground; and on the cross, when He was forsaken of God. He would have failed ere He had finished the cup of God's wrath, if ˙He had not been very God. But then He also could not have merited salvation.

2. The Mediator must be very God to give an infinite value to His merits.

The punishment of sin is an everlasting punishment. Suppose for a moment, that a real, righteous man had come. How long would such a mediator have had to suffer? FOREVER! i.e., that there never would have come an end to his sufferings; that the debt would never have been satisfied; that he never would have been able to say, "It is finished." But then true deliverance would have been impossible too. Satisfying for sin: payment to the uttermost farthing, is possible only because the Eternal God, in our human nature, has humbled Himself unto death. He was required to obtain an eternal righteousness through a suffering of short duration. And that could only be done by a Mediator Who is very, eternal God. The sinner can only become reconciled with God through God, (Acts 20:28).

B. And why did He have to be very man?
1. Because the justice of God demanded that the human nature, which had sinned, also make satisfaction for sin;
2. To be capable of suffering and dying.

1. God's justice will not suffer sin to be punished in a nature other than that in which it was committed. Man has sinned in soul and body, thus the Mediator must needs have soul and body, therein to satisfy God's justice. Adam's sin is imputed unto all

his descendants, and God's justice demanded that the Mediator be of Adam's generation in order that Adam's sin, for the elect's sake, could be imputed unto Him.

2. The Mediator had to be very man to be capable of suffering and dying.

The punishment of angels, which are spirits, is one thing, and the punishment of men, who have soul and body, is another. To bear their punishment, and thus to be capable of suffering and dying, it was necessary for the Mediator to be very man. The High Priest is taken from among men.

C. Why was it necessary for the Mediator to be righteous man, can be answered briefly: If He himself had had sin, He would not have been able to satisfy for others.

It should therefore be evident to all, that such a Mediator only can deliver, Who is very God, and a real, righteous man.

Qu. 15: *Who is that Mediator?*

Answer: Our Lord Jesus Christ, Who in one person is true God, and a real, righteous man.

Prove that the Lord Jesus is very God.

No reference is here made to the question whether the Son is of like essence with the Father and the Spirit, and thus very God; of that we hope to speak when speaking of God's Trinity. At present the question is whether Jesus the Nazarene, born in Bethlehem's manger; Who in all things was made like unto us, yet without sin, and Who died upon Golgotha, whether He is very God. The Jews refused to acknowledge this, and thousands of false Christians still deny it. It is indisputable, however, for the three Divine Persons have declared it.

The Father proclaimed it from heaven, Matt. 3:17 and 17:5.

The Son testified it of Himself, and His testimony is true, John 5:18; 10:33; Matt. 26:63.

The Holy Ghost declared it in both the Old and New Testaments, Ps. 2:7; Isa. 9:6; Micha 5:2; I John 5:20. He is Immanuel: God with us, Matt. 1:23; Isa. 7:14.

This testimony of the three Divine Persons is beyond contradiction. The Lord Jesus is very God; God was manifest in the flesh, (I Tim. 3:16).

He also is very man, with soul and body; man out of mankind.

He complained, "My soul is exceeding sorrowful, even unto death," Matt. 26:38, and, "Who his own self bare our sins in his own body on the tree," I Peter 2:24.

And He was born of the Virgin Mary: assuming her flesh and blood. In Luke 2 we are clearly told that He is the fully developed fruit of Mary. He partook of flesh and blood, Heb. 2:14.

Students, read carefully Art. 18 of our Confession of Faith.

Thus Christ did not bring His human nature of flesh and blood with Him from heaven. Then He would have had no fellowship with us, and then the sin of Adam could not have been imputed unto Him.

No, He became man out of mankind; a real, and . . .

Righteous man.

He had no original sin, and also no actual sin. He was that holy thing which was born of the Virgin Mary; not because Mary was holy and without sin, but because He was conceived by the power of the Holy Ghost, (Luke 1:35). He also was without actual sin; neither in deeds, nor in words, nor in thoughts did one sin cleave unto Him. He could say, "Which of you convinceth me of sin?"

It is therefore in accordance with God's Word, that this Mediator is the Lord Jesus Christ. He is very God, and a real, righteous man.

Still another particular requires our attention. The answer to Qu. 15 states that the Lord Jesus is God and man in one Person.

Therefore there are not two Mediators, one who is God and one who is man, but there is one Mediator between God and man, the man Christ Jesus, I Tim. 2:5. Otherwise, how would the suffering in the human nature have obtained a Divine value, and purchased an infinite righteousness? The Lord is, in one Person, very God, and a real, righteous man; one Person and two natures. Thus it was the Son of God that suffered, and the Son of God that died, but in our human nature. God hath purchased His church with His own blood, Acts 20:28. An everlasting righteousness is thereby acquired, in a suffering of short duration.

These natures are united in strict unity of one Person, in such a manner however, that each nature retains its distinct properties: God continued God, and man continued man. These natures are not intermixed, as taught by Eutichus. Neither do they ever become separated; not even in death. Nestorius wanted to separate the natures. The Synod of Chalcedon, in 451, spoke against both by stating that the two natures in Christ were in strict unity of one Person, being:

Without mixture and without change, . . . (against Eutichus);

Without division and without separation, (against Nestorius).

It should cause us to cry out, "Great is the mystery of godliness; God was manifest in the flesh," I Tim. 3:16. Have you become acquainted with this Mediator?

It being shown that only this Mediator can give deliverance, it is not difficult to follow the Compendium, where it is asked:

Qu. 16: *Could not the angels be our mediators?*

Answer: No; for they are neither God, nor man.

The angels therefore are not equal to the requirements demanded of the mediator. They are, together with mankind, the God-created rational beings, but are spirits and therefore have neither body, nor a human soul. The fallen angels shall suffer God's fierce wrath throughout an everlasting eternity in the lake of fire which is prepared for them. But they shall bear this everlasting punishment in their angelic nature. Man, however, is created with soul and body: has sinned in soul and body, and is subject in both soul and body to God's righteous judgments. To remove this punishment, the Mediator must have soul and body, and in these subject himself to the punishment due unto man, for the elect's sake. No angel therefore could have done this.

Furthermore, the justice of God could not suffer another creature to be punished for sin committed by man. All of mankind together have transgressed in Adam. The generation of man is damnable before God; satisfaction must therefore be made by man. Angels cannot be our mediators, even aside from the fact that no mere creature can bear the burden of God's wrath toward sin, and deliver others therefrom.

But the saints then? . . . .

Qu. 17 : *Cannot the saints be our mediators?*

Answer : No; for they themselves have sinned, and have obtained salvation by no other means, than through
this Mediator.

Saints are they who have been washed in the blood and by the
Spirit of Christ. Here upon earth they already become partakers
of the holiness of Christ by faith. The Lord Jesus said to Peter,
"He that is washed needeth not save to wash his feet, but *is clean
every whit.*" In conformity to which, Paul writes, "But ye are
washed, but ye are sanctified, but ye are justified in the name of
the Lord Jesus, and by the Spirit of our God," I Cor. 6:11.

However vile the people of God are in themselves, it is an holy
people, perfect in Christ. That caused the bride to say, "I am
black, but comely." And one day God's people shall put away
all sin and be perfectly holy; first according to the soul, when
at death it immediately enters heaven; and at the day of days,
also according to the body. It is to these saints in heaven that
this question refers: Can they be our mediators?

Indeed not! for these saints became partakers of holiness only
through Christ; they too were totally unclean by nature. Their
father was an Amorite, and their mother an Hittite, and to the
loathing of their person they too were cast out in the open field.
They were saved only through the Mediator Jesus. There is
nothing they can offer unto the Father to plead upon and bring
about a reconciliation. There is but one Mediator between
God and men, the man Christ Jesus, (I Tim. 2:5).

This testifies against Rome. They affirm that the departed saints
make an atonement with God for us through their merits and intercession; that the holy martyrs have wrought supererogatory good
works, which are imputed unto others to the forgiveness of sins,
through papal indulgences; consequently, the departed saints, together with Christ, are also our mediators before God, (see
VOETIUS - CATECHISM I). In this they injure the justice
of God, Who demands full satisfaction from the Mediator, and
herein they deny Christ, Who is the one and only Mediator.

Neither our works, nor those of others, can take away the punishment of sin, whether temporal punishment or eternal. We must
have a Mediator Who makes an atonement by satisfying God's

justice to the uttermost farthing of our debt. Whoever is destitute of this one and only Mediator, is destitute of everything that can restore him into the communion and favor of God. And the only Mediator is the Lord Jesus Christ, very God and very, righteous man. They shall be saved in Him, who are ingrafted into Him by a true faith.

Qu. 18: *Shall all men then be saved by the Mediator, Jesus as they are all condemned in Adam?*

Answer: No; but those only who receive Him by a true faith; as it is written, John 3:16, "For God so loved the world, that He gave his only begotten Son, that whosoever believeth in Him should not perish, but have everlasting life."

It is faith therefore which draws the line of separation here on earth, as it was predestination which made the separation before the foundation of the world. Christ is not a Mediator for all men. All are condemned in Adam. Adam represented his descendants in the Covenant of Works, but Christ the elect only in the Covenant of Grace. He therefore did not offer Himself for all men, but gave His blood only to atone for the sins of the elect. Neither does He pray for the world, but for them which were given Him of the Father, (John 17:9).

There is not a more abominable doctrine than that of universal redemption, originated by Pelagius, and disseminated by the semi-Pelagians, (like the Roman Catholics) and by the Remonstrants with renewed vigor. For their doctrine that Christ suffered and died for all men:

1.   DENIES the sovereign election of the Father;
2.   COUNTS the blood of Christ an unholy thing;
3.   DISAVOWS the saving ministration of the Holy Ghost;
4.   DENIES that man is dead in trespasses and sin.

1.   They deny the sovereign election of the Father.

Election has been accomplished in Christ, and it does not ascribe salvation unto all men, but unto them who are ordained thereto by the Father. The elect are given unto Christ, in order to be delivered by Him. And although He purchased an eternal righteousness of infinite efficacy and value, abundantly sufficient to expiate the sins of the whole world (Canons II, 3), yet this was the sovereign counsel, and most gracious will and purpose of God the Father, that the quickening and saving efficacy of the most precious death of his Son should extend to all the elect, for bestowing upon them alone the gift of justifying faith, thereby to bring them infallibly to salvation, (Canons II, 8). Christ's propitiatory sacrifice appertains to the elect. The Remonstrants deny this; they deny election.

2. They count the blood of Christ an unholy thing.

Did Christ then die for all men? . . . also for reprobates? for Esau? . . . Judas? Is Christ then dead in vain? (Gal. 2:21).

They who teach the doctrine of universal redemption, count the blood of Christ an unholy thing.

3. They disavow the saving ministration of the Spirit.

It is the Spirit that quickeneth, and applies Christ unto the elect. But universal redemption claims that this application is unnecessary, because it . . .

4. Denies that man is dead in trespasses and sin.

According to them, man has the ability to will and to believe. But Christ said, "Ye will not come to me," (John 5:40). The doctrine of universal redemption is incompatible with man's state of death.

This doctrine is an abomination, which seeks to destroy all the foundations of salvation.

To substantiate this doctrine of universal redemption, man even appeals to God's Word, as for instance, John 3:16; Romans 5:18; I Tim. 2:4; 2 Peter 3:9. How utterly unjust this is; for in not one single place is it written that redemption is accomplished for all men; then, indeed, not one would be lost; then there would be no hell. Salvation, however, is merited for the elect only; for them unto whom true faith has been given with which they receive Christ. Without faith is is impossible to please God.

Let us inquire somewhat into the several texts just mentioned.

In John 3:16, we read, "For God so loved the world, that He gave His only begotten Son." Now does that mean that God loved all men to salvation, and that then, notwithstanding this love, it is still dependent upon fallen man whether he will believe and inherit eternal life?

What manner of God's love must this Arminian love then be? for it is the Arminians who speak thus. They wrest God's Word, however, to their own destruction.

We read of "the world" in connection with the Mediator no less then ten times in Scripture. He is "the Lamb of God, which taketh away the sin of the world," (John 1:29). He is called the "Saviour of the world," (John 4:42). He is the "light of the world," (John 8:12). "God was in Christ, reconciling the world unto himself," (2 Cor. 5:19), etc.

Now what is meant by "the world" in all these texts? It definitely does not mean all men. The Lord Jesus himself said, "I pray not for the world, but for them which thou hast given me."

The love of God is to the elect world. And one day He will give unto them a new world; a new earth, wherein dwelleth righteousness, 2 Peter 3:13.

Thus John 3:16 positively does not teach a universal redemption.

Neither does Rom. 5:18, where Paul, (speaking of Christ's righteousness) says that "the free gift came upon all men unto justification of life."

In Romans 5, the two covenant heads are contrasted: Adam and Christ. All that are in Adam, signifies ALL MEN; All that are in Christ, are THE ELECT, given Him of the Father. Upon all men (in Adam) judgment came to condemnation by the offence of one; even so by the righteousness of one the free gift came (in Christ) upon all men (that are in Him, viz., THE ELECT) unto justification of life.

This is quite different from that taught by the Remonstrants with their universal redemption.

But, does not the Apostle say in I Tim. 2:4, that God will have all men to be saved?

Yes, so the Word reads. Now if this were to signify, . . . as the doctrine of universal redemption insists . . . that God will have every man, one by one, to be saved, why then doesn't it happen? God is surely able to perform His will?

But that has never been God's will! He has elected and rejected; loved Jacob, but also hated Esau; and that from eternity, out of pure sovereignty. The Arminians do violence to the Word of God, and distort it. Paul speaks of all manner of men; of kings, and all that are in authority, and of their subjects. He exhorts that prayers be made for those in authority. For God will have all men to be saved, i.e., all manner of men, of whatever class and station they may be. So therefore this text likewise offers no support unto the doctrine of universal redemption.

And, not to mention any more, what then is implied by the Apostle in 2 Peter 3:9, that God is not willing that any should perish, but that all should come to repentance?

It means to say, all who are included in the promise, and unto whom God is not slack concerning his promise.

There is not one text in the whole Bible which teaches universal redemption. This doctrine is contrary to the testimony of God. All men shall not be saved by Christ, as they perished in Adam. Christ offered himself for His people, Matt. 1:21; for His sheep, John 10:15; for His children, Heb. 2:10; for those given Him of the Father, John 17:2. And they, for whom He humbled Himself unto death, shall be saved. Them He raises up from the dead, and gives unto them faith by which they are implanted into Him, and receive Him. "But as many as received Him, to them gave He power to become the sons of God, even to them that believe on His name," (John 1:12).

The Lord cause this faith to be wrought in our hearts, that we may obtain salvation in Christ.

The receiving of Christ by faith is therefore not the fruit of our vineyard. Faith is the gift of God, and the receiving of Christ follows God's imputation of Him to us. First the Divine giving, and thereafter follows the receiving of Christ.

The Remonstrants, following in the footsteps of Pelagius, maintain that man possesses the ability to believe and to accept Christ. And many, (and then they call themselves Reformed), appear to be much inclined to Arminianism in practice. Among them there is nothing more commonly heard than the remark: "You must believe in Jesus. He died for sinners, and you must accept

Him." But a man can receive nothing, except it be given him from heaven, (John 3:27).

The receiving by faith is preceded by God's work of implanting into, and imputing of Christ. In his fear and distress Jacob sought refuge in the God of his father Abraham and of his father Isaac when Esau came to meet him; but after his wrestling with the angel at Peniel, when God had stripped him of his own righteousness and deprived him of his own strength, and he had become conqueror in God's strength, he erected there an altar at Shechem, and called it, "God the God of *Israel.*" Receiving followed the Divine imputing, and Jacob cried out, "That God is also *my* God."

That receiving is therefore also an embracing of the given Jesus. The English accordingly translate the word "accepted" in the text referred to, (John 1:12), into "received". "But as many as received Him, to them gave He power to become the sons of God." We must have a given Jesus. He merited salvation, but He also applies it unto them that are His.

But with this, the doctrine of universal redemption collapses entirely: because,

1st. Christ did not die for *all* men;

2nd. The receiving by faith is not of ourselves, but of Him

O, reject and cast far from you the false doctrine of universal redemption.

PART IV

Of the Essence and Summary of Faith

QUESTIONS 19-23

They only, who receive Christ with a true faith, shall be saved. All, however, have not this true faith. There is much counterfeit, therefore it is imperative to distinguish this saving faith from all that which resembles it.

The instructor treats of true faith in the following manner. He speaks:

1. Of the ESSENCE OF FAITH, (Qu. 19) being knowledge and confidence;
2. Of the SUM OF FAITH, (Qu. 20-42) briefly expressed in the Twelve Articles of Faith;
3. Of the PROFIT OF FAITH, (Qu. 43-47) viz., the justification of the sinner before God;
4. Of the AUTHOR OF FAITH, (Qu. 48) the Holy Ghost.

First, the ESSENCE OF FAITH is spoken of:

Qu. 19: *What is true faith?*

Answer: It is a *certain* knowledge of God, and of His promises revealed to us in the gospel, and an hearty confidence that all my sins are forgiven me, for Christ's sake.

By a true faith we understand that genuine faith which carries the imprint of the Holy Spirit. Saving faith has much imitation.

God's Word speaks of:

1. an HISTORICAL faith;
2. a TEMPORARY faith;
3. a MIRACULOUS faith;
4. a TRUE SAVING faith.

1. AN HISTORICAL faith is a bare assent to the truth. Agrippa had such a faith, unto whom Paul said, "King Agrippa,

believest thou the prophets, I know that thou believest." But with this faith, Agrippa remained a heathen, who was almost persuaded to become a Christian. Although it is so that an historical believer accepts Scripture as the truth, yet he receives it not unto salvation. He does not concern himself about his salvation.

It is to be feared, considering the carnal security and appalling insensibility of many who live under the Word of God, that they possess no more than an historical faith. Although this faith is certainly necessary, insofar as the knowledge of Scripture is indispensable, yet it is not sufficient. Therefore the historical knowledge of God's Testimony is distinguished in nature and essence from the knowledge of saving faith.

2. Temporary faith is more than historical faith. It is a professing of the truth for a time with some outward satisfaction. This outward satisfaction is not present with a lukewarm historical believer. In Scripture this temporary faith is likened unto seed which fell upon stony places, (Matt. 13). Here the seed has no deepness of earth. It springs up luxuriantly; in appearance it promises much; but when the sun is up, it withers away, and it bears no fruit.

Alas! Such is the temporary believer. Some temporary believers do have deep impressions of death and eternity in their consciences; for a time, they turn away from that open, outward service of the world, and join themselves to God's people. But after a short season, they return with the dog to his own vomit, and with the sow to her wallowing in the mire; God's saving work was never begun in them. Temporary faith has no root in Christ; it gives no fellowship with Him, no more than historical faith does. It therefore also leaves the sinner in his state of spiritual death. It furthermore cannot endure tribulation for the sake of truth. When tribulation or persecution ariseth, by and by the temporary believer is offended.

3. Miraculous faith is "a strong persuasion that a miracle will be performed either by, or on us," (Hellenbroek). It is not founded upon God's Word. It looks upon God's omnipotence, not His mercy. The case of the ten lepers is an example of this. All believed that Christ was mighty to heal them, and, on His Word, they showed themselves to the priest. But, nine desired

nothing beyond the miracle of healing the body; they took Christ
to be no more than a quack-doctor; they needed Him not to their
salvation. Only one of the ten returned to Jesus, and he was a
Samaritan. Their miraculous faith was a strong persuasion
that a miracle would be performed upon them.

In extraordinary times it pleased the Lord to give this faith
unto his servants, to perform miracles. The apostles, for instance, performed miracles in the name of the Lord Jesus. This
occurred especially to establish the truth which they preached.
Miraculous faith, however, is not unto salvation. "And though
I have all faith, so that I could remove mountains, and have
not charity, I am nothing," (I Cor. 13:2).

4. Of these various faiths, TRUE, "SAVING" FAITH is
essentially distinguished. This true faith is *"certain* (i.e., a
positive, not doubtful) knowledge of God, and of his promises
revealed to us in the gospel, and a hearty confidence that all my
sins are forgiven me, for Christ's sake."

True faith, therefore, embraces the grace which is in Christ.
In the state of innocence, Adam did not need *this* faith; in Christ
Himself, it was not necessary, and in heaven it shall no more be:
there it is changed into beholding. But in the hearts of God's
elect it is wrought and practiced. Alone through faith a lost
sinner is implanted into Christ; God's promises are opened unto
him, and he obtains the forgiveness of sins. This faith is not
an implicit faith without knowledge. Neither is there any
doubt in faith, no more than there is darkness in light.

How estranged from this true faith is Rome with her implicit and
doubtful faith.

In order to understand the instructor rightly, it is necessary
to distinguish between the essence and practice of faith. In the
essence of faith lies the knowledge and confidence that my sins
are forgiven me for Christ's sake. Without this knowledge and
confidence there is no faith.

But this does not imply that all God's people, in whose hearts
faith is wrought, are now assured of God's promises and the forgiveness of sins, although they enjoy the fruits thereof. They
obtain this assurance in the exercising of faith.

In the essence, however, both are present, otherwise it would not be possible, in the increase of faith, for them to be assured thereof.   In believers there also are often many doubtings; but not in faith itself; it is a *certain* knowledge and a hearty confidence, (John 17:3; Isaiah 53:11).

True faith then embraces all that God has revealed in the Gospel. This is briefly comprehended in the Twelve Articles of Faith. They form:

THE SUM OF FAITH

Qu. 20:   *What is the sum of that which God has promised in the Gospel, and commanded us to believe?*

Answer: That is comprehended in the Twelve Articles of the Catholic Christian Faith, which are as follows:

   1.   I believe in God the Father, Almighty, Maker of heaven and earth;

   II.   And in Jesus Christ, his only begotten Son, our Lord;

   III.   Who was conceived by the Holy Ghost, born of the Virgin Mary;

   IV.   Suffered under Pontius Pilate, was crucified, dead and buried, he descended into hell;

   V.   The third day he rose again from the dead;

   VI.   He ascended into heaven, and sitteth at the right hand of God, the Father Almighty;

   VII.   From thence he shall come to judge the quick and the dead.

   VIII.   I believe in the Holy Ghost.

   IX.   I believe an holy catholic church; the communion of saints;

   X.   The forgiveness of sins;

   XI.   The resurrection of the body;

   XII.   And the life everlasting.

These Twelve Articles also carry the name of the Apostolic Confession, because they are founded on the doctrine of the Apostles.

But did not the twelve Apostles then each compose one article?

Indeed not!   That is pure fiction. (Read Arnold Rotterdam's "Zion's Glory and Strength," Vol. I, pp. 115).

These articles were developed from the form of baptism. They contain the confession as to the three Divine Persons: Father, Son and Holy Ghost; for in the *one* Divine Essence, there are three Persons. This is seen in:

Qu. 21: *When you profess to believe in God the Father, and the Son, and the Holy Ghost, do you mean three Gods thereby?*

Answer: In no wise; for there is but one only true God.

At this point we enter into a discussion of the doctrine of the Holy Trinity.

There is one only God. "Hear, O Israel; the Lord our God is one Lord," (Deut. 6:4). Thus the Lord himself speaks also in Deut. 32:39, "See now that I, even I, am he, and there is no god with me;" and Paul, in I Cor. 8:6, "But to us there is but one God," and in I Tim. 2:5, "For there is one God."

The blind heathens are polytheists. They conceive of one God for the sun, and one for the moon; one for peace; and one for war, etc. So blind is man, even though he has an innate knowledge of God!

Dreadful heretics appeared also, who taught a dualism as to God. Besides other false Christians and heretics, our Confession of Faith mentions Marcion, who, as early as the year 140 A.D., taught that there was *one* merciful, and *one* just God; also Manes, from whom the Manichees descended, (Art. 9). The Church has justly condemned this heresy. There is but *one* God.

Qu. 22: *Why do you then name three, the Father, the Son and the Holy Ghost?*

Answer: Because God has so revealed Himself in His Word, that these three distinct Persons, are the only one and true God; and we also are baptized in the name of the Father, and of the Son, and of the Holy Ghost, (Matt. 28:19).

In the one Essence there are three Persons. This was denied by Praxeas, Sabellius and Samosatenus, who were deposed in the year 265 by the Synod of Antioch; Arius, condemned in the year 325 at Nice; and those who revived these heresies again at a later age, as Servetus, Valentius, Socinus, and others, (Conf. of Faith, Art. 9).

Can you prove the doctrine of the Holy Trinity from nature?

In no wise! For it is a mystery, not, indeed, contrary to, but still above the reach of nature. It is therefore also no evidence of the Trinity that a tree is a unit, and has root, trunk and crown; for they are three parts of one tree; in God, however, there is no uniting of parts, but in Him are three Persons. Likewise the three forms: water, steam and ice demonstrate nothing. For the Trinity has no more to do with forms, than with parts.

That there are three Persons in one Being cannot be proved from nature; but it can be proved from Holy Scripture.

Hellenbroek, as you have learned, gives the following texts as evidence:

A. From the Old Testament:
1. From texts where God speaks of Himself in the plural number, Gen. 1:26, "Let us make man in our image, after our likeness."
2. From texts where God and God, Lord and Lord, are distinguished, as in Ps. 45:7, and in Ps. 110:1.
3. From texts where the three Persons are expressly mentioned and distinguished, Ps. 33:6.
B. From the New Testament:
   The baptism of Christ; our baptism; and, I John 5:7, "For there are three that bear record in heaven, the Father, the Word, and the Holy Ghost: and these three are one."

These places of evidence could be increased by many; but rather, learn well the various texts mentioned.

The three Persons are one in Essence. There are not three Gods, but only one God. The complete Essence is in the Father; the complete Essence is in the Son; the complete Essence is in the Holy Ghost.

God is not "composed of", but "consists in" three Persons. Therefore it is not the case that the Father is 1/3, the Son 1/3, and the Holy Ghost 1/3 of the Divine Essence; No! not at all; but the complete Essence, is in each of these Persons, and yet there is but *one* God. This is far beyond our comprehension.

There is one Person of the Father; another of the Son; and another of the Holy Ghost; distinguished by their Personal Properties, or manner of subsisting. There also are essential properties, communicable and incommunicable, which the Persons have in common; but they are distinguished by the Personal properties.

The Father is self-existent; the Son is begotten of the Father, and the Holy Ghost proceeds from the Father and from the Son. The Eastern Church taught that the Holy Ghost proceeded from the Father only. In opposition to this, the Western Church properly stated: filio-que, i.e., also from the Son. Therefore He is called the Spirit of the Son, Gal. 4:6. The distinction of Persons is therefore not merely in name only, but there are three Persons in the Divine Essence. The Father did not assume our human nature, neither did the Holy Ghost, but the Son. From this the distinction of the three Persons is clearly evident.

We also should consider thoroughly that the Father is God, that the Son is God, and that the Holy Ghost is God. There is neither first nor last; the Father has never been without the Son, nor without the Holy Ghost. Neither is there any greater or lesser. The Son and the Holy Ghost are entitled to the selfsame honor and worship as the Father, (John 5:23).

How blasphemous then is the doctrine taught by Arius that the Son was the first-created being. The Son was not created, but eternal God; the firstborn of every creature, by Whom all things were created, (Col. 1:15). God, in eternity, was not a solitary God. He did not need the creatures, but fashioned them in time, according to His good pleasure. The doctrine of the Trinity is so important, that he who does not faithfully and steadfastly believe this doctrine, cannot be saved.

Unto each of these Divine Persons a work is particularly ascribed. The Father is the Creator; the Son is the Redeemer; the Holy Ghost, Sanctifier. This does not mean that the Son and the Holy Ghost were excluded from the work of creation, for by the Word of the Lord were the heavens made; and all the host of them by the breath of his mouth, John 1:3; Ps. 33:6. And sanctification is attributed also unto the Father and unto the Son, (Lev. 22:9; John 17:19; Eph. 5:26). But each work is particularly ascribed unto one of the Divine Persons. That is very evident from this, that the Son appeared and died in our flesh. By this He acquired deliverance, not the Father, nor the Holy Ghost, although these Persons are not excluded from the deliverance of the elect.

Thus the Father is the Creator.

This creation is spoken of in the last question of this Part:

Qu. 23: *What believest thou when thou sayest*: *"I believe in God the Father, Almighty, Maker of heaven and earth?"*

Answer: That the eternal Father of our Lord Jesus Christ, who of nothing made heaven and earth, and still upholds them by his providence, is my God and Father, for Christ his Son's sake.

This article therefore does not speak merely of creation. It confesses the eternal Fatherhood of God. He is "the eternal Father of our Lord Jesus Christ," who eternally begets the Son, and has chosen Him from eternity to be Mediator and Saviour.

Having already spoken of that, we now come to the creation.

What is creating?

Creating is to bring forth something out of nothing, "so that things which are seen were not made of things which do appear," (Heb. 11:3). "God calleth those things which be not as though they were," (Rom. 4:17). Creating is the work of God. All man can do is fashion: give different shapes unto that which exists. But if the raw material is lacking, the work of man comes to a standstill. God, however, created out of nothing. He brought forth all things by an omnipotent act of His will, (Rev. 4:11). Before God created, nothing existed outside of Him; not even a particle of small dust.

The creation did not therefore evolve from eternal matter in which existed a procreative faculty. Neither did God on the first day *create* matter with such a faculty. God is Creator, not alone the first day, but also the following five days.

Irreconcilably opposite to this stands the evolution theory of Darwin, traces of which can be found with the ancient Persians, Babylonians and Egyptians.

What manner of doctrine is it that all beings evolved out of matter; that man descends from an ape. Many rather believe such foolishness than bow before God's Word, which tells us, "In the beginning God created the heaven and the earth." God also created everything after its kind. Grapes are not gathered of thorns; man does not descend from an animal. Moreover, man is endowed with an immortal soul, and is entirely distinct from the animals. Only enmity against God's Word can bring forth such a doctrine as that of evolution.

God's honor requires the acknowledgement of the creation out of nothing. Dust must have been created; but what is created is not from eternity. God alone is eternal; and He created "in the beginning." Before that there was no beginning, no time. God caused time to be; He made evening and morning. Days, weeks and seasons are of Him. This circuit of time had its inception at the creation of heaven and earth, about six thousand years ago, and therefore not millions of years; the days of creation were not periods of countless ages; but ordinary days. The Lord states explicitly that we are to do all our work in six days, and are to rest on the seventh day, for in six days the Lord made heaven and earth, and rested the seventh day. The first, second and third days, when the sun did not yet rise and set, were also ordinary days, in which God gave and withheld light. But how then can we account for the physical changes in the earth?

Were not thousands of years necessary for the fossilization of trees, etc. etc.?

Any who wish to appeal to this, should ask himself:

1. What has God created *in* the earth?
2. What changes were caused by the curse, wherewith the ground was cursed for our sake?
3. What were the consequences of the deluge?

Let us adhere to God's word that teaches us that God created heaven and earth in six days.

In a moment did God create the chaos, and then He gave form to the same. The angels were probably created the first day, for when the foundations of the earth were laid, they already were in existence, (Job 38:6, 7). In one moment they were brought

forth in their countless number, thousands of thousands, and ten
thousand times ten thousand. Among them is neither man nor
woman; no angel is born. God gave existence to them all at the
same time in His creative act, so entirely different from the
creation of one human being from whom all mankind descended.

Do you know the days of creation?

Compare the first with the fourth day; the second with the
fifth; the third with the sixth. What a glorious agreement!

On the seventh day God rested from all His work which He
had made. No, God was not weary of creating; "the Creator of
the ends of the earth, fainteth not, neither is weary," (Isa. 40:28).
He needs no rest, as does man: The resting of God refers to His
enjoying Himself in His work, from which He withdrew not His
hand. His resting is the sanctifying of the day, and He blessed it.
Of Him and through Him and unto Him are all things. In the
creation His eternal power and Godhead are clearly seen, (Romans 1:20). The Lord hath made all things for Himself, that is,
to His glory, (Prov. 16:4).

The creation is described as:

a.   The work of the FATHER: . . .Acts 4:24; and I Cor. 8:6;

b.   The work of the SON: . . . John 1:3; Eph. 3:9; Col. 1:16;

c.   The work of the HOLY GHOST: Gen. 1:3; Ps. 33:6.

Each of the three Persons has His particular work in creation.
Nevertheless the creation is more particularly the work of the
Father.

His work is also that of:

PROVIDENCE

He upholds all things by His providence, as we read in the
answer to Question 23.

The word "providence" appears but once in the Bible; the
verb "provide" often. When Abraham prepared to offer Isaac, he
said, "God will provide himself a lamb for a burnt offering," in
Gen. 22:8, and Abraham called the name of that place: "The Lord
will provide."

The word "provide," in reference to God, is also used in Hebrews 11:40. In these instances, this word, meaning "forsee," does not only signify that God did see and know beforehand, but also that He supplies what is necessary. That is also the meaning of the word providence.

In the Bible, providence is called:

GOD'S REIGN ....Psalm 93:1
GOD'S ORDINANCES ....Psalm 119:91
GOD'S HAND ....Acts 4:28
GOD'S WORKING ....Isaiah 28:29
GOD'S CARE ....I Peter 5:7
GOD'S UPHOLDING ....Hebrews 1:3

(see J. Vermeer, Catech.)

In Providence we distinguish three acts, viz.: Preservation, Concurrence and Government.

Preservation is the almighty power of God, whereby He continues all things in their being. It is the continual operation of the Father, (John 5:17). No creature is of himself, nor can exist of himself. Every creature must be preserved.

This preservation is mediate, or it is immediate. Moses was preserved without means by God on Mt. Horeb for forty days; but the Lord sustained Israel in the desert by means; as He did Elijah at the brook Cherith, and with the widow at Zarephath. At times the Lord is also pleased to work miraculously in the mediate preservation, especially of His people. That we might observe it more.

The Concurrence of God is the almighty power of God, from which flows the strength for all His creatures' motions and operations. At birth we do not receive all the strength necessary throughout our lifetime, but God supplies us every moment with strength for every act. We cannot raise our hands, nor move our tongue, independently of God. But at one time every creature shall give account before God's tribunal of the use made of this strength.

The Government is the almighty power of God whereby He directs everything to a certain determinate end: all things, great and small, good and evil, Eph. 1:11. It includes heaven and earth; rational and irrational creatures, Job 28:1; Acts 17:28.

Does the influence of God's governing providence also extend to sin?

Yes, He directs it, although He does not work it. He performs the counsels of His own will through it. Consider, for instance, the selling of Joseph as a slave into Egypt; "but God meant it unto good." He overruled this evil.

The hardness of Pharaoh's heart, (Ex. 9:12), and the perverse spirit which God gave in the midst of the heathen kings, (Isaiah 19:14), are also evidences of this. God reigns also over Satan, who can accomplish nothing outside of God's will, (Job).

Thus the providence of God is not an unintelligible operation, like the fatalism of the Mohammedans.

Deism is also condemned therein, in which creation is presented as a clock which runs down of itself. Job speaks of this opinion as of the way of wicked men, (Job 22:15).

The doctrine of providence is of vast significance. It teaches us to be thankful in prosperity; patient in adversity; and confidently trusting for the future.

O, that we might sincerely believe that God reigns supreme, and that we might give ourselves into His hand. That would be the fruit of true faith, that the eternal Father of our Lord Jesus Christ, is my God and Father.

That the Lord may work this faith in our hearts, to entrust ourselves unto Him for time and for eternity.

PART V

Of the Son and Our Redemption

QUESTIONS 24-31

Having attended in Part IV to the subjects of the Divine Trinity, the Father and our creation, we now advance to the second division of the Twelve Articles of Faith.

These articles are divided into three parts:

The first speaks of

GOD THE FATHER, AND OUR CREATION;

The second speaks of

GOD THE SON, AND OUR REDEMPTION;

The third speaks of

GOD THE HOLY GHOST, AND OUR SANCTIFICATION.

We are now to discuss the second of these, viz., of the Son and our redemption.

OF THE NAMES OF THE MEDIATOR

In dealing with this second division of our Twelve Articles, the Compendium speaks first of the names of the Mediator which are used in the Twelve Articles in reference to Him.

These names are: Jesus Christ, Only Begotten Son, and Lord.

Qu. 24: *What believest thou when thou sayest: "And in Jesus Christ his only begotten Son, our Lord?"*

Answer: That Jesus Christ is the eternal and only son of the Father, co-essential with God the Father and the Holy Ghost.

The Mediator is the Son of God. We have already established this beyond doubt in Part III from the testimony of the three Divine Persons, the Father, Son and Holy Ghost. He, who was born in Bethlehem's manger, Who walked as man in the midst of Israel, Who died upon Golgotha, was greater than all men. He not only was man but also God; the eternal and only Son of the Father, co-essential with the Father and the Holy Ghost. He did not first become God's Son when He assumed our human nature from the Virgin Mary. That was the heretical teaching of Socinus, who died in 1604, and who denied the Son's existence from eternity. His heresy was revived by the Modernists. They speak of Jesus as of a good man, worthy to be emulated. But the Lord Himself testified that He is the Son of God. Moreover, the Jesus of the Modernists is not worthy to be heard or followed. The Godhead of the Son was denied long before the time of Socinus, by Arius, who was condemned by the Synod of Nice in 325.

It is in opposition to this denial of the Mediator's Godhead that the Compendium teaches that He is the eternal and only Son of the Father, co-essential with the Father and Holy Ghost. In the Ecumenical Creeds, Athanasius states plainly and distinctly: "The Father is eternal, the Son is eternal, and the Holy Ghost is eternal. So the Father is God, the Son is God, and the Holy Ghost is God."

The Mediator is the Son of God; the Uncreated; God from eternity to eternity. He was, before He came in Bethlehem's manger. "But when the fulness of the time was come, God sent forth His Son, made of a woman, made under the law," (Gal. 4:4). In order to be sent forth, He had to be; and He was the true God from all eternity. The only begotten of the Father, (John 1:14; 3:16; I John 4:9).

The elect are called children of God, but they are not children of God by virtue of an eternal begetting; not by being co-essential with the Father and the Holy Ghost; but by adoption for Christ's sake. He alone is God's eternal and only Son, with the Father and the Holy Ghost, true God. He is the eternally begotten, of whom the Father spoke, "Thou art My Son, this day have I begotten Thee," (Ps. 2:7). He can save His people therefore, because He is very God, the only begotten of the Father. But for that purpose He also had to become man.

Qu. 25: *Do you not believe that He also became man?*

Answer: Yes: for He was conceived by the Holy Ghost, and born of the Virgin Mary.

He assumed our human nature by the conception of the Holy Ghost. Therefore He is called, "that holy thing" that was born of the Virgin Mary; for that reason only. Not because Mary was immaculate, as taught by idolatrous Rome. How could she be immaculate? She was born like unto every other creature; she also was included in that truth, "Who can bring a clean thing out of an unclean? Not one," (Job). The Virgin Mary was not without original, nor without actual sin. She was saved by Christ through grace alone. Personally, Christ was excluded from the imputation of Adam's covenant breach; He had neither original sin, nor actual sin, because He was conceived by the power of the Holy Ghost. Yet He became man out of mankind; the fully developed fruit of the Virgin Mary; her flesh and blood, the true seed of David after the flesh, belonging to Adam's race, and therefore He complied with the demands required of the mediator. (See Part III).

Consequently Christ has two natures: He is God and man. For He remained very God, also after His birth of Mary. But He is *one* Person: the Second Person in the adorable Divine Essence.

Qu. 26: *Is His Godhead then changed into humanity?*

Answer: No; for the Godhead is immutable.

So says the Lord Himself in Mal. 3:6, "I am the Lord, I change not." Would God cease to be God? Impossible. The Son remained what He was: very God and eternal God.

But do we not read in Phil. 2:7, that He made Himself of no reputation?

This does not signify that He ceased to be God, or that His Godhead was changed into humanity; but this making Himself of no reputation refers to the manifestation and to the use of His Divine glory and majesty.

He, the Son of God, came in the *form* of a servant. Being in the form of God, He thought it not robbery to be equal with God. But He became His Father's servant out of sovereign, eternal love, (Isa. 42:1). And in this form of a servant He came upon earth, concealing His Godhead behind the veil of His human nature. And also in this form of a servant, He laid aside the use of His Divine attributes, so that He, although being the Almighty, was bound as one powerless, and nailed to the cross. He is the Omniscient, yet it is written of Him, that He increased in wisdom.

But He continued very and eternal God; unchanged according to His Godhead, and undiminished in glory.

Qu. 27: *How is He then become man?*

Answer: By assuming the human nature into a personal union with His divine.

Of this we have already spoken also, when the requirements were treated which are demanded of the Mediator. (Part III). God's only-begotten Son, the Second Person in the adorable, blessed Divine Being, assumed our human nature . . . *not a human person.* Then there would have been two persons and two mediators. That was not so. It was for that very purpose, that the Divine Person, God Himself, brought the sacrifice, and suffered and died in our human nature. And to that end the Son of God assumed from the Virgin Mary that which all of mankind have in common, viz., our nature: soul and body. This nature He assumed from the Virgin Mary. He took upon Him not only the body, but also a real human soul, that He would be very man. For since the soul was lost as well as the body, it was necessary that He should take both upon Him to save both.

Tht Anabaptists deny His true birth of the Virgin Mary. According to them, He passed through the Virgin Mary as water passes through a trough. But then He would not be very man out of man, and therefore could not have borne and taken away the sins of His elect. To bear the sins of His people, He had to be of the true seed of David; a fruit of the womb of the Virgin Mary; made of a woman. (See Art. 18, Confession of Faith).

Qu. 28: *Did He then bring His human nature from heaven?*

Answer: No; but He took it on Him of the Virgin Mary, by the operation of the Holy Ghost, and is thus become like unto his brethren in all things, sin excepted, (Hebrews 2:17 and 4:15).

If He had brought His human nature from heaven, He would have stood outside of our human race; then the sin of Adam, which is imputed only unto his descendants, could not have been imputed unto Him. Then He could not have taken away sins, and saved His people from them.

No; He did not bring His human nature from heaven, but He assumed the same from the Virgin Mary.

This incarnation was:

(a)   The work of the FATHER: He prepared Him a body, Hebrews 10:5;

(b)   The work of the Son: . . . He was made flesh, John 1:14,

(c)   The work of the Holy Ghost, Who wrought in Mary, Matthew 1:20, and Luke 1:35.

The Son alone, however, assumed our human nature. He is become like unto us in all things, sin excepted. He had no sin, but otherwise He was like unto His brethren in all things. His human nature was not like unto that of the state of innocence. In that state, man neither hungered nor thirsted; Adam did not weep, as long as there was no sin; neither did he become weary. As he came forth from God's hand in creation, man was also immortal. But Christ hungered and thirsted; He was weary of His journey; He wept at the grave of Lazarus; He died on the cross. In all things He became like unto His brethren, that He would be able to succour them in all things: when they hunger and thirst: when they are weary, and weep by their dead: when they must struggle with death. He is the compassionate High Priest. God's eternal Son, the second Person of the Divine Essence, is become man; the Mediator, praiseworthy unto all eternity. O, that we might behold Him by faith. He is fairer than the children of men.

Qu. 29: *Why is He called Jesus, that is, Savior?*

Answer: Because He saves His people from their sins.

Jesus is the *personal name* of the Mediator; the name Christ is His official name. He is moreover called by many names in Scripture which reveal unto us His glory and His might. Consider Isaiah 9:6. "His name shall be called Wonderful, Counsellor, The Mighty God, The Everlasting Father, The Prince of Peace." (see also Isaiah 7:14).

But His personal name is JESUS. That name was given by the angel upon Divine command, ere He was born. In the age of types and shadows, that name was already used. According to Heb. 4:8, Joshua, who is called Jesus in this place, had the same name.

Joshua was a type of Christ; Joshua the son of Nun, as well as Joshua the High Priest. But in its *full* significance, only the Mediator carries the name Jesus.

The name Jesus means: Saviour, as the angel declared to Mary, "For He shall save His people from their sins." To save is to deliver from the greatest evil, and make a partaker of the supreme good. The Lord Jesus delivers His people from sin, and restores them into fellowship with God.

He wrought this salvation by meriting and *applying*. He not only acquired salvation, but He applies it also. Without this applying, not one of Adam's children would become partaker of this salvation wrought by Him. Christ is the complete and only Savior by doing both. Therefore it is improper for anyone to call himself by this name. This is done by the Jesuits, who in fact deny that Christ is the only Savior. The Lord Jesus alone is able to save us, by grace, without any merits of our own. Everything needful to salvation is received by God's people from Him, Whose personal name is Jesus. Salvation is in none other.

We are directed to this in the following question, which asks,

Qu. 30: *Is there no other Savior?*

Answer: No; for there is none other name under heaven given among men, whereby we must be saved, than the name of Jesus, Acts 4:12.

Whatever names we may consider: to whomsoever we may want to flee for refuge, "None of them can by any means redeem his brother, nor give to God a ransom for him," Ps. 49:7. O, that we might then renounce all creatures, to seek and to find salvation in this Jesus alone. Neither our God-fearing parents; nor God's servants: nor the saints in heaven can do one thing towards our salvation.

He alone is the Savior, Who in truth is Jesus.

Moreover, He is the Christ.

Qu. 31: *Why is He called* CHRIST, *that is, anointed?*

Answer: Because He was anointed with the Holy Ghost, and ordained by God the Father, to be our chief Prophet, our only High Priest, and our eternal King.

The name Christ signifies *anointed*. It is a Greek name, which Andrew informs us, in John 1:41, is interpreted *Messias* in the Hebrew. Under the Old Testament, Prophets, Priests and Kings were anointed. Elijah anointed Elisha to be prophet, (I Kings 19:16). The anointing of priests is described in detail by Moses. No one was to make an oil like unto it, after the composition of it, for common usage; it was solely for the priests' use.

Scripture further gives many instances of the anointing of Kings. Saul, David, Solomon, etc., were anointed to their offices. Saul with a breakable earthen vessel, for the kingdom was to be taken from him; David with the unbreakable horn, because his kingdom would endure unto all eternity, viz., in Christ.

What did this anointing signify?

1st. Appointment to the office;

2nd. Qualification for the office.

The signification of the appointment to the office appears plainly in I Sam. 16.

Samuel was sent to Bethlehem to anoint one of the sons of Jesse to be king in the place of Saul. It was not known to Samuel who among these sons God had intended for Israel's throne; the Lord had only said to him, "I have provided me a king among his sons."

At the sacrifice that Samuel brought at God's command, that the anointing of David would remain hidden, the sons of Jesse passed by Samuel. He looked upon their outward appearance, and said, "Surely the Lord's anointed is before him." But what did the Lord say, now and again? "I have refused him." "Neither hath the Lord chosen this." Samuel had to anoint the chosen of God.

This chosen one, however, was not among the seven sons which Jesse caused to pass before Samuel. David, apparently so slightly regarded in his father's house that he, even at this very special occasion as Samuel's coming, had been left by the sheep, was then called; and of him the Lord said, "Anoint him, for this is he." God's chosen had to be anointed.

This anointing not only expressed the appointment to the office, but also the *qualification*. God would give in like manner His Spirit in large measure, to qualify his chosen for the office.

Christ then, is appointed and qualified. He is appointed from eternity, and qualified in time. In Prov. 8:23, Christ says, "I was set up (or anointed) from everlasting, from the beginning, or ever the earth was." His qualification, however, took place in time, having assumed our human nature; for to be Mediator, He must not only be God, but also man.

The anointing of Christ took place, however, neither with breakable vessel, nor horn. Such an anointing, howsoever abundant, was in measure. But the Lord Jesus is anointed with the Holy Spirit, without measure. "The Spirit of the Lord God is upon me; because the Lord hath anointed me," Isaiah 61:1.

He was herewith anointed unto three offices. Christ was Prophet, Priest and King. David was King and Prophet, (Acts 2:30); Melchisedec was King and Priest, (Heb. 7:1); Christ has three offices.

As Prophet He teaches the way of salvation. He does this by His Word and Spirit. We understand not the way of salvation; All the children of God shall be taught of the Lord, (Isa. 54:13). To this administration, He only is able, because He was in the secret councils of God. He is the Word, (John 1:1); the great Prophet, (Luke 7:16); of the Father made unto us wisdom, (1 Cor. 1:30).

Christ performed the Prophetic administration under the Old, as well as under the New Testament; as well prior to and during, as after His walk on earth. He taught under the Old Covenant, He proclaimed the counsels of God unto Patriarchs and Prophets in visions, dreams, verbal admonitions, appearances, by Urim and Thummim. He bestowed the Holy Spirit, and caused His Word to be recorded, (2 Peter 1:21). The Socinians, who deny the Godhead of Christ, refuse to acknowledge this administration of Christ under the Old Testament. But how could man, also under the Old Covenant have the eyes of his understanding enlightened, without the prophetic administration of Christ? He administered His Prophetic office from the very beginning, and that in a twofold manner:

a.   He gave the special revelation, written in the Bible, and,

b.   He enlightens the hearts of the elect.

When He was upon earth, He taught in person. He entered upon His prophetic administration publicly at His baptism by John, (Matt. 3:16, 17). The Father not only declared, "This is My beloved Son," but also sealed His Prophetic administration, saying, "Hear Him." Christ makes manifest the manifold wisdom of God, (Eph. 3:10). In Him are hid all the treasures of wisdom, (Colossians 2:3). He expounded the law; applied the prophecies; He established His doctrine by signs and wonders, (John 5). He taught as one having authority, and not as the scribes. In all this, however, He neither brought a Gospel other than had formerly been preached, nor did He amend the law, as the Socinians and their followers insist upon. Neither did He abrogate the law, as the wicked Antinomians teach. He satisfied the law for His people, disarmed it of its curse, and glorified it perfectly and causes His people to walk according to it.

Christ was qualified for the Prophetic administration, being anointed with the Holy Spirit without measure. He needed not to ascend to heaven to be instructed, as the Christ-denying Socinians foolishly prattle.

After His resurrection, for yet forty days; the Lord taught his disciples; but not the world. And since He ascended to heaven, He still teaches by His Word and Spirit, and by means of His servants. The Apostles and Prophets and Evangelists were extraordinary; the Pastors and Teachers are ordinary office bearers, (Ephesians 4:10-13).

Christ is Priest after the order of Melchisedec. There are two priestly orders; of Aaron and of Melchisedec. It was after the order of Aaron that the sons of Aaron were priests; but Christ could not be Priest after this order, for He was not of Aaron's family; not even of the tribe of Levi. He was Priest after the order of Melchisedec.

This Melchisedec, although born of man, had no descent as priest. He was an only priest, and since he was this by God's sovereignty, he had an eternal priesthood. Christ is an only priest and an everlasting priest. He only has offered the sacrifice of atonement, and He lives forever to intercede for His people. Aaron's priests were but types of Christ.

How does He execute His priestly office?

By offering sacrifice, and making intercession.

Christ has offered. The blood of bulls and goats, as were offered by the priests, could not take away sin. For that purpose did Christ offer Himself, (Heb. 7:27). He made His soul an offering for sin, (Isa. 53:10). Peace is made through the blood of His cross, (Col. 1:20), and the conscience is purged, (Heb. 9:14). Christ offered this sacrifice for His people; not for Himself, as taught by some erring spirits. It was not necessary that He should offer for Himself, but His sacrifice was for His people, fully satisfying for their sins, and, for theirs alone.

Thus the Lord Jesus, as the great High Priest, intercedes only for them which were given Him of the Father, (John 17:9). For them He interceded while on earth and now in heaven, in the sanctuary, not made with hands. In the great day of atonement under the Old Covenant, the High Priest entered into the most holy place to pray. Christ has entered into heaven; there He liveth forever to intercede for His people. He is the Intercessor for them who are His; (I John 2:1) the Advocate. But He is not an advocate of intercession only, but also of reconciliation. He is not an advocate who only pleads the case, but pleads it to a successful conclusion; for His intercession is a demanding: "Father, I will, that they also, whom thou hast given me, be with me where I am," (John 17:24). For His intercession rests upon His satisfaction. Thus He carries the twelve tribes of Israel upon His heart, mindful of His Church day and night.

Without His intercession in heaven, Christ's work as Mediator would be unfinished. "For if He were on earth, He should not be a priest," (Heb. 8:4). O, what a comfort for God's people lies in the Priestly Intercession of Christ! They are also blessed by the only High Priest with temporal, spiritual and eternal blessings.

As King, Christ delivers, protects and rules His people. He delivers and protects them from Satan, the world and sin, and rules them by His Word and Spirit, that they walk in His ways. He is King for ever; and one day shall receive all praise and homage from His people.

Christ was typified by the kingly office in Israel. For this purpose the kingly office had to come to them, although Israel, in its ignorance, realized it not, when they desired a king, rejecting God who was their King.

But after Saul, God in His favor gave unto them His servant David, who was a type of King Jesus, (Jer. 30:9). That Christ was King, He Himself testified before Pilate, (John 18:33-38). But His kingdom is not of this world. It was not, therefore, transferred upon the Pope, as if he were a vicar of Christ. This kingdom is spiritual and eternal; a heavenly kingdom.

The King . . . the subjects . . . the laws . . . the privileges, all here is spiritual. Here Christ reigns with all power which is given unto Him in heaven and in earth. The whole world, and even the devils, are subject unto Him, and are powerless against Him.

O, that Christ make these offices within us glorious with power unto enlightenment, reconciliation and deliverance.

He causes His people to need Him continually in the administration of these offices.

PART VI — A.

Of the States of the Mediator
QUESTIONS 32-34

The states of Christ determine the relation in which He stands with respect to the justice of God. Regarding this justice, but two relationships are possible, i.e., that of a debtor, and that of one acquitted.

So there are but two states of the Mediator. Because of the sins of the elect, He was the debtor to His Father's justice in the state of His humiliation; and He stands acquitted in the state of His exaltation.

To the profound depth of this humiliation, whereby He had to satisfy fully for the sins of His people, He descended by way of five steps. The degrees of His humiliation are:

1. His humble birth;
2. His sufferings;
3. His death;
4. His burial;
5. His descending into hell.

Out of this deep humiliation, Christ again is exalted by way of four steps. The degrees of His exaltation are:

1. His resurrection;
2. His ascension;
3. His sitting at the right hand of God the Father;
4. His coming again to judgment.

It is of these states that PART VI speaks. First of

THE STATE OF HUMILIATION

In the previous lesson, the birth of Christ was spoken of. This birth, considered by itself, belongs with the qualifications of the Mediatorship. For the deliverance of lost sinners, it is necessary to have such a Mediator, Who is together very God and a real, righteous man. The humble birth, however, is the first step of the Mediator's humiliation.

He, the King of kings and Lord of lords, for Whom no suitable palace could be built, was born in a manger; more humble and destitute is inconceivable. At birth He already descended into the state of profound misery in which His people were. He came to suffer and die.

Qu. 32. *What then hath Jesus Christ done to save us?*

Answer: He hath suffered for us, was crucified and died, was buried and descended into hell, that is, He suffered the torments of hell, and thus became obedient to His Father, that He might deliver us from the temporal and eternal punishment due to sin.

The suffering of the Lord had its inception at His birth. He bore the burden of God's wrath all the time He lived on earth. He was wrapped in swaddling clothes and laid in a manger; He underwent the painful circumcision; He fled before the murderous sword of Herod. A poor and humble bringing up was His portion. He was tempted of the devil in the desert; He was weary; He hungered; He wept at the grave of Lazarus. In a word, His whole life upon earth was a life of suffering, terminating in His death.

Toward the close of His life upon earth, this suffering increased greatly. In the Garden of Gethsemane, where He bore the burden of Adam's trespass committed in Paradise, He lamented, "My soul is exceeding sorrowful even unto death." He was surrounded with sorrows. The wrath of the Father descended upon Him; the sins of His people distressed Him. Satan beset Him with all the powers of hell. Yea, so sorely was Christ afflicted, that His sweat became as it were great drops of blood falling down to the ground. If He had not sustained His human nature by His Godhead, it would have succumbed.

The blessed Surety was aware of this suffering. He knew that the hour was come; He spoke of it to His disciples. Notwithstanding, He willingly went forth upon the path of suffering, because He loved His own unto the end. With His disciples He sang hymns of praise. He did not enter into death like a helpless martyr, but as the Lamb to satisfy God's justice, and as the Lion of the tribe of Judah, to bruise Satan's head, being confident of His victory.

And with what death did He die? He was crucified!

He was condemned to this death judicially by Pontius Pilate. When Herod desired to kill Him, He fled. He likewise evaded the Jews when they attempted to stone Him, or cast Him ·down headlong from the brow of the hill whereon their city was built. It was necessary for Him to be condemned by the judge, in order to set His people at liberty in the justice of God.

The death of the cross was a despicable, painful and an accursed death. The crucifixion as executed by the Romans was unknown among Israel. The Israelites did hang one who had been put to death, on a tree, to express the abomination of his sin, but the Romans crucified them alive. One crucified hung as a reproach on the cross, rejected by the earth, while the heavens were closed unto him. They died under the most excruciating pains.

The death of the cross further was accursed of God. So Moses declared in Deut. 21:23, "For he that is hanged is accursed of God." His dead body was not permitted to remain all night upon the tree, that the land be not defiled by his curse. Christ, therefore, dying the death of the cross, was made a curse, thereby redeeming His people from the curse of the law, (Gal. 3:13).

And on the cross HE DIED!

Death was a necessary part of His suffering. In the fall of Adam, His people had, with all of Adam's descendants, subjected themselves to death; and to redeem them from death, Christ needs must die. Albeit He cried out, "It is finished," *before* He died, in it He included His death. Immediately after speaking these words, says John (John 19:30), "He bowed His head, and gave up the ghost."

In like manner Christ spoke already before being taken captive, in John 17:4, "I have finished the work which thou gavest me to do," but these words definitely do not imply that the suffering and death which was now at hand were superfluous. Likewise His last cross-words, "It is finished," did not exclude His death. As it is appointed unto man once to die, but after this the judgment, so Christ likewise must needs die to bear the sins of many, Hebrews 9:27.

Christ died a three-fold death. The spiritual death is the separation from the favor of God. However, Christ was not subjected to the consequences of this death, as the losing of God's image and the bondage of sin and Satan. But He was forsaken of His Father on the cross. His soul was exposed to God's wrath that is kindled against the whole human race, and cannot be divided. It was also under the burden of sin and of Satan's afflictions. It was in these Christ entered into spiritual death.

He also died a temporal death. Soul and body were parted, although He saw no corruption. (Ps. 16).

And, lastly, Christ was subjected to eternal death. This is an everlasting suffering of punishment in hell. To redeem His elect from everlasting punishment, Christ's agonies, before His death, were of no less intensity than those to be suffered by the reprobates in everlasting fire.

In His suffering of short duration, Christ bore the full wrath of God, although He at no time became the object of God's wrath, as reproachfully stated by the Socinians. But He, also in this full outpouring of God's wrath, remained God's beloved Son, in Whom He was well pleased. The Father found a supreme delight in the offering which Christ brought in His indescribable suffering.

The Socinians deny that Christ bore the punishment. They say that God forgives sin without satisfaction being made. But then God would renounce His justice; and that is impossible for God to do.

The Remonstrants say, that Christ was subjected only to temporal death, which was accepted by a propitious appraisement of God, as satisfactory. But in the justice of God there is no acceptance save only that which makes full satisfaction to the demands of the law. So only by being subject to this three-fold death could Christ remove the curse. Thereby He satisfied His Father's justice, (2 Cor. 5:21); disarmed the law of its curse, (Gal. 3:13); and reconciled the elect with God, (Rom. 8:1).

The Lord Jesus confirmed His death with His *burial*.

Joseph of Arimathea and Nicodemus laid His body in a new tomb hewn out of a rock, wherein never man before was laid. Their request for Jesus' body was granted by Pilate only after he was assured that the Lord truly had died. Thus Christ confirmed with His burial that He indeed had died. He thereby also sanctified the grave for His people. There the wearied are at rest unto the day of resurrection. As typified by Jonah, the Lord reposed in the grave three days and three nights; from Friday evening until Sunday morning. Parts of days are reckoned as whole days.

Did His descending into hell then follow?

No! This descending into hell took place before His death. Rome and the Lutherans consider this descending into hell as the first step of His exaltation, but it belongs to the state of His humiliation. Luther reasoned that Christ descended into hell after His death, to demonstrate His victory. But for this reason Christ never would have descended into hell. Rome errs far worse. They assume heaven to have a limbus or porch; here the faithful of Old Testament days were to have been held captive until Christ came to deliver them. And that, say they, took place when the Lord descended into hell following His death.

This presentation conflicts entirely with the Truth:

1. *No* limbus or porch to either hell or heaven exists. The thief on the cross entered heaven directly with Christ; and if there was *one* sinner who indeed came short, supposing that man himself must do penance for his daily sins, then it certainly was this thief. But Christ took away all his sins, and admitted him into heaven directly.

Futhermore, in Rev. 14:13 we find written, "Blessed are the dead which die in the Lord *from henceforth.*"

So, the existence of forementioned limbus or porch being proven to the contrary, Christ likewise could not descend thereto.

2. The believers who lived in the days of the Old Testament, entered *heaven* when they died. They entered therein on this ground, that the Lamb was slain from the foundation of the world. It was not necessary for them to await Golgotha's death.

Thus the descending into hell does not signify that Christ went to hell in person, but that He suffered the agonies of hell . . . . *before* His death.

The placing of this article after His burial is done to cast a comprehensive light upon the Lord's suffering and death.

In Christ's humiliation there was more than the eye of man

could discern; in it was the bearing of all the suffering in hell unto an everlasting eternity that His people had subjected themselves to. This suffering of the pains of hell was upon Christ, and took place before He died. To this profound depth does the Heidelberg Catechism expound this descending into hell. The Westminster Catechism does not go beyond Christ's abiding in a state of death; but the Heidelberg Catechism leads us further into the meaning of the descending into hell, although both reject the teachings of Rome, and also the interpretation given to this article by Luther.

This suffering was wholly and solely in the human nature, as is spoken of in the next question.

Qu. 33: *In which nature hath He suffered this?*

Answer: Only in His human nature, that is, in soul and body.

God cannot suffer and die; the Divine Person however has accomplished this suffering in His human nature, i.e., in soul and body.

It is not at all spoken to Christ's disparagement (as Rome foolishly asserts) when we teach that Christ suffered also in His soul. This we are told in Scripture. The Lord cried out, "My soul is exceeding sorrowful, even unto death." We have sinned in soul and body; in soul and body Christ had to suffer, to redeem His people according to both soul and body. He bore our sins in His body on the cross.

Qu. 34: *What hath then His Godhead contributed thereto?*

Answer: His Godhead, by its power, in such wise strengthened the assumed human nature, that it could bear the burden of God's wrath against sin, and deliver us from it.

Read again what was said on this article in Part III. No mere creature can bear the burden of God's wrath against sin to the end.

Christ furthermore had to give an infinite value to His merits. Therefore He had to be very God, although He did not suffer in His Divine nature.

In His humiliation, the Lord Jesus satisfied Divine justice unto perfection; the debt of the elect was paid by Him unto the uttermost farthing. But then, He could no longer be held captive by death.

The state now to be spoken of is:

THE STATE OF EXALTATION

God hath highly exalted Him, (Phil. 2:9). This exaltation was essential. If Christ had remained in a state of death, how then would one single sinner have arisen out of the grave of sin? . .and also how then would death have been swallowed up in victory? It is for this reason that Paul states Christ's exaltation to be greater than His death, (Rom. 8:34).

Moreover, He not only had to merit salvation, but also apply it; and He could send His Spirit for this purpose only after He was glorified, (John 16:7). Furthermore, the Mediator of the New Covenant had to appear before His Father, (Heb. 9:11, 12). The exaltation of the Lord Jesus was foretold, as in Ps. 8:5; Ps. 89:19; Isa. 53:12. It also was typified in Joseph, (Gen. 41 and 42); and in David, who both were exalted after being humbled; and in Solomon, whose greatness was a type of Christ's glory.

For this exaltation the Lord Jesus Himself petitioned, John 17:5. He desired the glory which He had before the world was. He had covered the glory of His Godhead with the veil of His human nature; but this had to beam forth in all its glory in His Mediatorship, that all men should honor the Son, even as they honor the Father, (John 5:23). As He was a debtor to God's justice while in the state of humiliation; in the state of His exaltation He stood acquitted. Therefore He is crowned with honor and glory, and unto Him, as Mediator, is given that which was wanting in His humiliation, viz., the glory which He had ere the world was. Unto Him a name is given which is above every name, (Phil. 2:9). For He hath put all things under His feet, (I Cor. 15:27).

In this exaltation, both natures of Christ remained inseparably united. Although the body was glorified, it retained the human attributes, as the Divine nature retained the Divine attributes.

The first step of this exaltation was the resurrection.

We hope to speak of the degrees of this exaltation in the following lesson.

Of the Degrees of Christ's Exaltation

QUESTIONS 35-38

The first step of Christ's exaltation is His resurrection.

Qu. 35: *Did Christ then remain under the power of death?*

Answer: No; but He rose from the dead the third day for our justification, Rom. 4:25.

The resurrection is the first step of exaltation of the Mediator. Lutherans and Roman Catholics consider the descending into hell as the first step of Christ's exaltation, but, as we already have mentioned when dealing with this article, this belongs to the state of humiliation.

The resurrection was foretold, and to the prophecies uttered under the Old Testament dispensation, the New Testament often refers; as, for instance, Acts 2:27-31; see Ps. 16:10.

The Lord Jesus Himself, during His sojourn upon the earth, spoke of the resurrection, John 2:19; Matt. 12:40; 16:1-4; and also of the three days He would be in the grave.

Examples of Christ's resurrection are the budding staff of Aaron, (Numbers 17:8); Samson's departure from Gaza, (Judg. 16:3); Jonah, (Matt. 12:40). No human eye has actually seen the resurrection itself.

Yet there are many witnesses to it:

1. The testimony of angels, Luke 24:5, and Matt. 28:7;

2. The tangible falsehood of the keepers, who reported among the Jews that they had fallen asleep. Slept at such an important post?...all at one time?...so fast asleep that the disciples could roll back the stone uninterruptedly? . . . slept so long, that the disciples could remove the body and bury it elsewhere? . . . and this all then could have taken place while the designated thieves nevertheless testified later in the temple of the resurrection without

being haled before the Jewish council and accused of their enormous crime?

The falsehood of the keepers is surely a strong testimony of Christ's resurrection.

3. The many appearances of the Lord prove His resurrection. The Lord has revealed Himself unto His disciples by many infallible proofs to dispel their unbelief and allay their fears. Women and disciples became witnesses of the resurrection; Thomas especially is a proof thereof, (Matt. 28; John 20).

4. Paul powerfully evinces the truth of Christ's resurrection when he states in I Cor. 15:6 that "He was seen of above five hundred brethren at once; of whom the greater part remain." They could still be asked about it.

5. The Lord was seen of Paul himself.

Thus the infallible proofs of the resurrection are manifold, and should stop the mouths of all gainsayers.

In the resurrection, Christ's soul and body were again united; not His natures, for they were not separated, even in death. The same body which was laid in the grave rose again, and put on immortality. The Lord showed the print of the nails, Luke 24:39; and John 20:20. The same body was glorified. After the resurrection it was no longer subjected to death, Rom. 6:9; Rev. 1:18. Furthermore, it was a real body that could not penetrate the stone of the grave, neither closed doors, as the Lutherans and Roman Catholics assert, as if the body had become spiritual.* The body of the resurrection was the selfsame body; to convince His disciples of this, the Lord permitted them to touch Him, and He ate before their eyes, although He no longer needed meat or drink.

The resurrection is ascribed to the three Divine Persons:

1. It is the WORK OF THE FATHER, Ps. 16:11.

Maintaining the injured justice of the essence of God, God the Father demanded satisfaction; but He also acquitted Christ eternally. Thus the resurrection is the justification of Christ and in Him of all His people, and this raising up from the dead is ascribed to the Father, John 17:5; Acts 2:32, 33; Rom. 4:25.

---

*See Article 19, Confession of Faith.

2. The resurrection is the WORK OF THE SON.

He had power to lay down His life and power to take it again. In the resurrection Christ destroyed him that had the power of death, (Heb. 2:14). Thus the resurrection is unto them that are His, not only for their justification, but also for victory.

3. The resurrection is the WORK OF THE SPIRIT.

As the Spirit of holiness, the Holy Spirit separated Christ forever from death, and has sanctified and glorified completely, Him Who was made sin, (Rom. 1:4).

The resurrection of Christ, therefore, is the work of the three Divine Persons.

Christ was buried on Friday evening; He rose again on Sunday morning. Thereby He sanctified THE FIRST DAY of the week as the Lord's Day, (Rev. 1:10), and the day of rest for the New Testament, Acts 20:7).

The resurrection of Christ, therefore, contains:

a. The JUSTIFICATION of all His elect;

b. Their SANCTIFICATION in Him;

c. Their VICTORY over all enemies;

d. Their RESURRECTION from the dead;

e. Their PLEDGE OF A BLESSED RESURRECTION.

God's people are raised out of a spiritual death, (Eph. 2:1). Their death likewise no longer is a chastisement, but a passing to life eternal, (Hos. 13:14; I Cor. 15:26). Eternal death is abolished. The resurrection of Christ is a pledge of their blessed resurrection. The righteous shall be raised to eternal life, to praise their God and King, according to both body and soul forever.

Blessed are they who have their portion in Christ's resurrection.

The risen Mediator ascended into heaven after He first had showed Himself for forty days unto His disciples.

The second step of His exaltation is His ASCENSION.

Qu. 36: *Where is Christ now, as to His human nature?*

Answer: He is ascended into heaven, and sits at the right hand of God the Father; that is, exalted in the highest glory, far above all creatures, Eph. 1:20, 21.

The Lord powerfully convinced His disciples of His resurrection during the forty days before His ascension. After His resurrection He no longer showed Himself unto the world, as He did before His death. Neither was He continually with His disciples as heretofore; He prepared them for His ascending into heaven.

Speaking to the women at the sepulchre, He said, "I ascend unto my Father, and your Father; and to my God, and your God." For His Church another life was being prepared; a life of spiritual communion; a beholding by faith, and not by sight, 2 Corinthians 5:7. All knowing after the flesh would fall away, (2 Cor. 5:16). The resurrection was the beginning of Christ's glorification, and withdrew Him from the world, that He would be glorified with the glory which He had before the world was.

Christ entered into this glory through His ascension. David prophesied of this ascension in Ps. 24; 47; 68. Enoch, (Genesis 5:24), and Elijah, (2 Kings 2:1), were types of it, and the apostles were eyewitnesses to it, (Mark 16:19; Acts 1:9). Christ was entitled to this glorification. He Who was made a little lower than the angels, had to be exalted exceedingly, and crowned with glory and honor, (Heb. 2:9).

As Highpriest, He must needs enter into the holy place not made with hands; and, as King, triumph there forever. He had to open the doors of heaven for His people: the doors which had been closed by sin. He is gone up with a shout, with sound of a trumpet, (Ps. 47:5). The angels received Him with a voice of rejoicing, (Ps. 118:15); and the saints before the throne filled heaven with songs of jubilant praise, when they saw their Lord and King enter into His glory. O, what a glorious meeting this must have been for them.

The ascension is spoken of in Scripture in various ways. It states that:

He was taken up, Acts 1:9;

He ascended, Eph. 4:8;

He is made higher than the heavens, Heb. 7:26;

He entered into the holy place, Heb. 9:12;

He is gone to the Father, John 14:12;

He left the world, John 16:28.

The ascension had three characteristics.   He ascended Actually; Visibly; and Locally.

1.   The ascension of Christ has been an actual ascending into
heaven; a taking of our human nature, according to both body and
soul, into heaven.   When angels appeared in human form on earth,
they often took upon them a material body; not a real human
nature, with a soul, nor a body born of man.

By their departure from earth, their bodies would turn to dust
again; it ascended not into heaven.   But the Lord Jesus took the
assumed human nature, soul and body, into heaven.   His ascension
was an actual ascending into heaven.

2.   This ascension was performed visibly.   Not one creature
was an eyewitness to the resurrection, but the ascension took
place in full view of His disciples.   These disciples looked
stedfastly toward heaven as He went up, until a cloud received Him
out of their sight.

3.   The ascension was local, i.e., the Lord Jesus brought
soul and body from one place on earth, viz., from the Mount of
Olives, to another place, in the third heaven, which God has
created for His throne.

It is especially to refute the Socinians, that we must insist
that Christ entered into heaven with His own soul and body; the
selfsame body in which He died and ascended.

In this Luther erred also.   This great reformer taught the
omnipresence of Christ's human nature; that His omnipresence
was placed at the full disposal of His human nature at the ascension.   But then Christ is not truly ascended into heaven.
Luther applied this doctrine in the Supper, teaching Christ's
corporeal presence by, with and in the visible tokens.   It becomes apparent that the most richly endowed are but human beings.   How could Luther possibly decline to such an extremely
absurd error!   He changed the human nature into the Divine.

Christ is no longer upon earth according to His human nature.
It was expedient for His Church that He should go away, John 16.

"Me ye have not always," so He Himself spoke, in John 12:8. This must be maintained not only to refute the error of Luther, but particularly against Rome.

The Roman Catholic priests claim to change the bread and wine of the Popish mass into the body and blood of Christ, and then offer Him in the mass, (see Part X). The Lord, however, will remain in heaven until He comes again in the day of judgment, (Acts 1:11). It was therefore not on earth, but in heaven that He was seen of Stephen, (Acts 7:55, 56), and of Paul, Acts 9:4, 17, and of John, Rev. 1:10-18.

In His ascension Christ opened the heavens for His chosen people; He alone opened them. No creature accompanied Him; not even the saints that came out of their graves after His resurrection.

Not a word is mentioned to this effect in Scripture; and Rome's abominable doctrine, that those whom Christ delivered from purgatory by His descending into hell, ascended with Him into heaven, is absolutely contrary to Scripture, (see PART VI-A). To what extremes does Rome deviate from the truth!

Furthermore, Christ ascended into heaven but once. The Lutherans and Romanists fabricated a visible and an invisible ascension of the Lord; the invisible ascension repeating itself frequently.

This ficticious story is connected with their doctrines of consubstantiation and transubstantiation; so one lie must cover the other. There is, however, but one ascension and one coming again to judgment, (Acts 1:9-11).

Christ entered into heaven, and sits there at the right hand of the Father, to the benefit of His people, and as an earnest of their entering into heaven according to both soul and body.

Qu. 37: *To what end is He there so highly exalted?*

Answer: Particularly that He might from thence govern His Church, and there be our Intercessor with the Father.

This lesson then speaks of the sitting at God's right hand as the third step of Christ's exaltation. This expression must be understood spiritually. God is a Spirit, and He therefore has neither a body, nor a right hand.

But among men, the right hand is a place of honor, as Solomon caused a seat to be set for his mother on his right hand, (I Kings 2:19). Unto Christ is given the place of highest honor, not in front of, but in the midst of the throne, (Rev. 5:6). Thus the Mediator obtained the glory which He had before the world was, (John 17:5). He is exalted to the highest majesty, (Heb. 1:3). At God's right hand, it is said of Christ that:

> He is.................................Rom. 8:34
> He sits ....Heb. 1:3
> He stands.........................Acts 7:55

He is said to sit at God's right hand, to express that He finished and perfected His work. His standing points to the exercising of His dominion, whereby He is ready at all times to succor His people.

This perfect glory was promised Christ, (Ps. 110:1); it was also typified by the exaltation of Joseph, and in the bringing of the ark to Zion, Ps. 47; Ps. 68. God's justice required this exaltation, (Phil. 2:9), and it is to the benefit of His Church.

From heaven He administers His offices; He teaches and leads and governs His people. He gives His servants, pastors, and teachers, (Eph. 4:11). He plucks those whom He redeemed with His blood, out of the power of Satan, and treads upon His enemies, Ps. 2:3-9. He poured out His Spirit, as promised, Isa. 44:1-3; John 16:7. It is Christ's will in heaven to be worshipped as the true God. It is improper for any to worship the human nature in the abstract, like Luther, who deified this nature. It belongs unto Christ to be worshipped as the true God. Once He shall reveal His full majesty and glory when He comes again to judge the quick and the dead.

Qu. 38: *Is He not with us then even unto the end of the world, as He hath promised us?* Matt. 28:20.

Answer: With respect to His Godhead, majesty, grace and Spirit, He is never absent from us; but with respect to His human nature, He remains in heaven, until He shall come again to judge the quick and the dead.

That shall be at the last day, for Christ shall not appear on earth before that time. The contrary to this, however, is taught by the Pre-Millenialists, propagators of the millenium. They say that:

1. Christ will be corporeally present on earth, for a period of a thousand years;

2. The departed saints shall then be raised from the dead;

3. Jerusalem then shall be the centre of this glorious ecclesiastical state.

This doctrine is to be totally rejected. The Lord Jesus shall come again but once, and that shall be at the great judgment-day. Until then He shall remain in heaven.

How dreadful shall this coming again of the Lord be.

"Behold, He cometh with clouds; and every eye shall see Him, and they also which pierced Him." (Rev. 1:7).

Dreadful shall that day be for them; they shall be cast out, both soul and body, into the lake of fire. Whereas God's people shall inherit the Kingdom, prepared for them from the foundation of the world.

O, that we all may be prepared for this awe-inspiring coming again to judgment, so that we may look forward to it without fear, and learn to say with the Bride of the Lamb.

"COME, LORD JESUS, YEA COME QUICKLY."

PART VII

Of the Spirit and of the Church

QUESTIONS 39-42

The Compendium speaks first of the Father and our creation, (Part IV), then of the Son and our deliverance, (Part V and Part VI), and now is to speak of the Spirit and our sanctification.

Qu. 39: *What do you believe concerning the Holy Ghost?*

Answer: That He is the true and coeternal God with the Father and the Son; and that He being given to me of the Father, through Christ, regenerates me and leads me into all truth, comforts me, and will abide with me forever.

The Spirit is thus true and eternal God; co-essential with the Father and the Son. We prove this by His names; by His attributes; by His works and by His honor.

He is specifically called God in contradistinction to man. See Acts 5:4, where Peter says to Ananias: "Why hath Satan filled thine heart to lie to the Holy Ghost? Thou hast not lied unto men, but unto God."

Of the attributes of the Spirit, we will mention only the omnipresence, (Ps. 139). God only is omnipresent; this attribute then proves that the Spirit is the true God.

This is manifested by His Divine work of creation, Ps. 33:6, and the Divine honor which belongeth unto Him, viz. to be baptized and blessed in His name, Matt. 28:19; 2 Cor. 13:14.

Therefore the Spirit is not a mere power or attribute of God, as taught by Socinus; He is the true God: the third Person in the Divine Essence, Who proceeds from the Father and from the Son. Unto Him is ascribed understanding and will. The Spirit searcheth all things, yea, the deep things of God, (I Cor. 2:10), and divideth to every man severally as He will, (I Cor. 12:11). That can never be said of a power or attribute, but only of a Person.

Therefore the Spirit is also called, "another comforter," in John 14:16, Whom Christ sent on the day of Pentecost.

This, then, is the Spirit who is given unto the elect. He regenerates them, i.e., from death He makes them alive; and therefore regeneration preceeds faith, (Canons III-IV: 12; see also Part II). The Holy Spirit further gives growth to him that is regenerated, and by faith causes him to become more and more conformed to God's image; in this respect regeneration issues from faith.

It is in this sense that regeneration is spoken of in Article 24 of our Confession of Faith. These two Doctrinal Standards are therefore not conflicting. At Dort our fathers circumscribed the essence of regeneration; whereas this Article of our Confession, which treats of sanctification, describes the manifestation of regeneration.

Regeneration is the work of the Holy Spirit in the hearts of the elect. He makes them partakers of the life of Christ. He guides into all truth, and makes it known unto salvation, (John 16:13). The Spirit also comforts God's people. He is the Comforter that shall abide with them until the last day. He intercedes for His people in their hearts, like Christ intercedes for them in heaven.

So the Church of God has an Advocate in heaven, and also one in their heart.

In regeneration a true, spiritual fellowship is wrought with Christ, and also with all His members. Thus those regenerated are not independent, but they form a spiritual body. This body is called the Church, which is spoken of in the next question.

Qu. 40: *What believest thou concerning the holy catholic church?*

Answer: That the Son of God gathers by His Word and Spirit out of the whole human race, those, who are chosen to eternal life, to be a church to Himself; of which I believe I am, and always shall remain a living member.

By "*The Church*" we therefore do not merely understand an assemblage of people, but the congregation of the elect; a holy congregation of true Christian believers, all expecting their salvation in Jesus Christ, (Art. 27, Confession of Faith). There is but one Church, (Song of Solomon 6:9), but this one Church has two parts; one part already triumphs in heaven: one part is yet militant upon earth. This Church upon earth can again be considered as: an organism and as an institute, or, as it is also called, the invisible and the visible church.

But this is not to be understood as if these could be separated, . . . as if God's quickened people were here, and yonder a dead carcass, which then would be the visible church. To the contrary; the work of the Holy Spirit in those regenerated manifests itself in the visible church. But as no grain grows without chaff, so the visible revelation of the Church is likewise not without chaff. And so it shall ever remain upon earth.

Who wanted to have a church composed entirely of true believers?

Jean de'Labadie, minister at Middleburg in 1666, was one of them; but he was sadly disappointed. He acted contrary to Scripture.

The Lord Jesus knew very well what Judas was, yet He permitted him to be one of the twelve. Should we then be able to purge the visible church of tares and chaff? That shall one day be done by the Lord Himself.

Here the church is like a company of wise and foolish virgins; as the field which brought forth tares and wheat; as the net containing fish, both good and bad. Thus we have to consider the visible church according to God's Word. It is misleading to deal with all who are in the visible church as living members of Christ. Nevertheless, the elect alone are the true members, as stated in the answer: "that I am and always shall remain a living member thereof." These living members are the elect, gathered together by the Lord Himself.

Election and *Rejection* together are called:

PREDESTINATION

What is predestination?

In a special sense, it is said of Christ that He is the elect of the Father, (Isa. 42:1) We confine ourselves, however, to the predestination of creatures, and then it is: The decree of God concerning the eternal state of rational creatures. The rational creatures are angels and man. Thus there is an election and rejection of angels as well as of man.

As regards the angels, I Tim. 5:21 speaks of their election: and Jude 6 of their reprobation. And as concerns man, Scripture speaks in many places of both the election and rejection of man. God not only loved Jacob, but also hated Esau, (Rom. 9:13). He hath appointed some to wrath, as well as others to obtain salvation, (I Thess. 5:9). There are vessels fitted to destruction, as well as vessels prepared unto glory (Rom. 9:22, 23).

And this election and rejection is out of pure sovereignty. All moving or conditional causes outside of God, whether in the performing of good or evil by the creature, are hereby totally excluded. God did not elect any because of foreseen faith or good works, nor reject any because of evil works. Predestination is not an act of mercy or justice, but of the sovereignty of God. It is the Father's good pleasure to give you the kingdom, Luke 12: 32; (see also Matt. 11:26; Rom. 9:22, 23; Eph. 1:5) With this, Pelagians and Socinians are condemned; likewise Roman Catholics and Remonstrants, all of whom deny the absolute sovereignty of God's decree.

With the Remonstrants, who were followers of Arminius and therefore also called Arminians, our fathers engaged in a heavy conflict in the early part of the 17th century, until the Synod of Dort, (1618-1619), proclaimed their condemning sentence upon the Remonstrants.

The Remonstrants teach that they, whom God foresaw would, of their own will, believe and convert themselves, are chosen to salvation. They maintain that man is independent of God in deciding his state for eternity. God was considered dependent on man; He has but to await what men, whose state of death the Remonstrants deny, will do: believe or not believe; persevere or turn aside. With this God-dishonoring doctrine, predestination is no longer a foreordaining of persons, but only a regulation in regard to the state, which man would then choose for himself.

But, as we have already seen, God's Word speaks of predestination of persons known of God by name, (Rom. 9:13).

Against the corrupt theses of all who deny the sovereignty of God's decree, our fathers maintained:

1. That God's sovereign good pleasure is the only reason of the foreordination. It did not even happen on account of Christ, but *in* Him, Who on that account is the Head of the Church, and in Whom all are that shall be saved; wherefore He could represent them in the Covenant of Grace, like Adam represented all in the Covenant of Works, who were in him.

2. It is impossible that the creature, which is brought forth in time, can be the cause for what was decreed in eternity.

3. Faith and good works are fruits of election, and not causes of it.

4. All things happen by virtue of God's decree, and man therefore does not make himself to differ, (I Cor. 4:7).

The pure doctrine of God's sovereignty was maintained unanimously by all the Divines at Dort, against the Arminians. However, all did not do this in precisely the same manner. A point of difference existed among these orthodox men.

This difference is indicated by the terms:

Supra- and Infra-Lapsarians

The sovereignty of predestination is especially maintained by the *Supra-Lapsarians,* whereas the *Infra-Lapsarians* wanted to lay more emphasis upon man's responsibility.

They differ in the moral order which they make in God's decrees. There is no chronological order in these decrees, and both of these factions, also called "Above- and Below-the-Fall-Zealots," therefore teach that predestination is from eternity. At the Synod of Dort, both have signed the Doctrinal Standards with respect to the point in question, and consequently neither one was condemned.

Yet there is a difference, and it consists in this, that the *Supra-Lapsarian* teaches predestination to have taken place prior to the decreeing of the creation and the fall; and the *Infra-Lapsarian* takes the viewpoint of an election out of the fallen human race.

The order which each maintains is this:

SUPRA-lapsarians	INFRA-lapsarians
PREDESTINATION	CREATION
CREATION	THE FALL
THE FALL	PREDESTINATION

HERE Predestination stands above the Fall; therefore: ABOVE-THE FALL-ZEALOTS

HERE Predestination stands below the Fall; therefore: BELOW-THE FALL-ZEALOTS

The infra-lapsarian also places the Fall in the foreknowledge of God, and not in His decree. (See Part II).

Neither of these parties places anything in man, nor does either one of them make God the author of sin.

The election of angels did not take place, as must be conceded by the infra's, out of fallen angels. Why then teach that this *did* take place out of fallen mankind.

In predestination, man is considered as not yet created, nor fallen. Predestination is the decree of God to glorify Himself in rational creatures, both in mercy and in justice. To that end He decreed to create them, and, as concerns man, He included them in the fall.

Observe therefore this distinction:

(a) In predestination, man appears as not yet created and fallen;

(b) In the Covenant of Redemption, man (although not yet existing) appears in God's decree as being created and fallen.

Both factions mentioned, however, maintained predestination to be the eternal, sovereign, unchangeable decree of God, determining the eternal state of rational creatures.

This decree is from eternity, (Eph. 1:4). Neither Satan, nor the world, nor sin can cause the foundation of salvation of God's people to be removed; that lies beyond their reach.

Furthermore, election and reprobation are unchangeable, (Rom. 9:11; 2 Tim. 2:19). No elect creature can perish; no reprobate can ever be saved.

Is it then not immaterial, how man lives?

No; for God's decrees give no license to commit sin. God has also decreed the means which serve to accomplish His good pleasure; the neglect of which shall aggravate our judgment.

Moreover, God's decree is not revealed to us, and no man can therefore make any use of it, (Deut. 29:29). The mocker, the profane, the lover of sin, despises (like Esau) the sovereignty of God; but shall also experience that God shall one day mock when their fear cometh, (Proverbs 1:26).

Would it not be better then, seeing the misuse many make of it, to remain silent regarding the doctrine of predestination?

No, indeed not. God's Word does not keep silence of these things. In Rom. 9, Paul defends God's sovereign good pleasure. If we had to refrain from speaking of the principal parts of the Reformed doctrine because of the abuse levelled against them, then soon not one of them could any longer be taught.

Moreover, predestination serves to magnify God's sovereignty, and to abase man to the lowest. In foreordination lies also the main ground of salvation. The doctrine of predestination is the source of comfort for God's people; therefore that people shall rejoice in it with unspeakable joy, (Luke 10:20).

The Lord gathers the elect unto Himself as a Church, by His Spirit and Word. Not alone by the Word, but by the effectual ministration of Spirit, Who works by means of the Word.

Therefore each should give diligence to search God's Word, and be present at the proclamation of the Gospel. By means of the Word the Lord gathers His Church. Now this Church is said to be: HOLY, CATHOLIC, CHRISTIAN.

God's people are holy in Christ; in Him they are perfect, and by Him they are sanctified. The Church is catholic, since the Lord has redeemed His own to God by His blood out of every kindred, and tongue, and people, and nation, (Rev. 5:9); therefore this name appertains unto the true Church alone, and not unto Rome, who delights to call herself the catholic or universal church, but does so unjustly. It is a false church, which our fathers spoke of as, "The anti-christian Rome." "The "catholic church" is the true Congregation of the Lord. It is Christian because it partakes of Christ's anointing. And these names apply also to the visible church, because it reveals before the eyes of the world how God is glorified in the hearts of His elect.

The visible church is therefore also to be known and distinguished from all false churches.

Qu. 41: *Where doth He gather His Church?*

Answer: Where God's Word is purely preached, and the holy sacraments administered according to the institution of Christ.

Those are the marks of the true Church. Rome appeals to the antiquity of its church; but Satan's kingdom is also old. This is the thing that matters, that God's Word is purely preached according to the mind of the Spirit. Inseparably connected therewith is the proper administration of the sacraments, whereof we hope to speak in Part X. If these marks are lacking, the Church of Christ is not there, regardless of what they may allege to sustantiate their claims. In this respect, let every one be fully persuaded in his own mind, and join himself to the true Church of the Lord.

In order to maintain the purity of Word and sacrament, it is imperative for the Church to exercise discipline. (See Part X).

Great are the benefits which the Lord bestows upon His Church.

Qu. 42. *What benefits doth Christ bestow on His Church?*

Answer: He grants her remission of sins, the resurrection of the body, and eternal life.

Christ has obtained these benefits for His elect, and unto them He applies them. Not therefore unto all who belong to the visible church, but unto the Church which He has obtained for Himself through His blood. Their sins are forgiven in justification, whereof Part VIII speaks.

The second benefit which is spoken of in Question 42, is the resurrection. All of mankind who have died, shall once be raised from the dead. The sea and earth shall give up their dead, (Revelations 20:12, 13). They that have done good and they that have done evil shall come forth unto the resurrection, (John 5:29), while they, who shall yet be living on earth at Christ's second coming, shall be changed in a moment, in the twinkling of an eye, (I Cor. 15:51, 52).

When this coming again of the Lord shall be is not known to man. Of that day and hour knoweth no man, but the Father only, (Matt. 24:36). We cannot, therefore, calculate when that day shall be, yea, neither may we even attempt it.

Man, notwithstanding, has repeatedly prohesied that the world would pass away on a certain day and year, determined by them. But they all have been put to shame. But the day of the Lord will come as a thief in the night. Neither shall the Lord come on earth before that day. The Pre-Millenialists, therefore, who await Christ to reign on earth during the millenium, err grievously.

Although the exact time has not been revealed to us, yet the day of judgment shall surely come, and then the dead shall be raised.

The resurrection shall be a resurrection of the selfsame body wherein the soul dwelt while on earth. The union of soul and body, which were separated by death, shall then be restored, nevermore to be broken. However many centuries the body shall have been returned to dust, it shall in no way hinder the resurrection thereof; neither of those that were devoured by the beasts of the earth; nor of those whose bodies were surrendered to the flames, and consumed to ashes.

We cannot fathom this mystery, but God's Word teaches us this emphatically, and to this Word we must submit oursleves, notwithstanding that many reject it, and refuse to accept the resurrection.

There already were those in the days of Christ's sojourn on earth, who denied the resurrection. They were the Sadducees, (Matt. 22:23). But the Lord Jesus refuted their vain and foolish questions to their shame. Paul also contradicts those who say there is no resurrection. The Apostle teaches in 1 Cor. 15, that the resurrection is of so great importance, that all of salvation itself is dependent upon it. For, "if there be no resurrection of the dead, then is Christ not risen," vs. 13. "Yes, and we are found false witnesses of God; because we have testified of God that He raised up Christ; Whom He raised not up, if so be that the dead rise not," vs. 15. "And if Christ be not raised, your faith is vain; ye are yet in your sins," vs. 17. "Then they also which are fallen asleep in Christ are perished," vs. 18.

With many clear proofs, Paul shows in these words the vast importance of the resurrection. The Apostle moreover takes an example from nature which proclaims the resurrection, saying in the 37th verse, "and that which thou sowest, thou sowest not that body that shall be, but bare grain, it may chance of wheat, or of some other grain." And, behold, he who sows wheat, reaps wheat; who sows barley, reaps barley. "God gives to every seed his own body," vs. 38. Thus also a human body is sown, and a human body is raised up. Paul calls him, who denies this, a fool. With all their learning, they are fools, who deny the resurrection. The selfsame body that died shall be raised again.

It was upon this that Job's hope was founded, when in faith he proclaimed, "And though after my skin worms destroy this body, yet in my flesh shall I see God," Job 19:26.

God's justice also requires that sin shall be punished in the same body wherein sinners committed the same, "that every one may receive the things done in his body, according to that he hath done, whether it be good or bad," (2 Cor. 5:10).

That body, however, shall have different qualities. It shall be immortal and incorruptible. The body wherein we lived on earth could not subsist, neither in hell, nor in heaven. But the Lord shall raise up a spiritual body, i.e., a body that is immortal, and adapted for the everlasting abode into which it shall enter with the soul.

The substance of the body shall not be spiritual, because it remains a material body, else it would no more be a body, but it shall no longer be subject to corruption, nor in need of meat and drink. And God's elect shall receive a glorified body, like unto the glorious body of Christ, (Philippians 3:21).

O, how great shall be that day of resurrection!

Judgment shall immediately follow the resurrection. This judgment shall be pronounced by Christ, Who shall appear visibly before all men, with His many thousands of holy angels. Every eye shall see Him, and they also which pierced Him, (Rev. 1:7). How fearful shall be that looking upon the despised Nazarene.

Then the holy angels shall . . . . .

(a) Gather the righteous;

(b)   Sever the wicked;

(c)   Cast the damned into the lake of fire and brimstone, (Matt. 13:30, 49, 50).

Before judgment is pronounced upon Satan and all the wicked, Christ shall set His elect at His own right hand, (I Thess. 4:17). In the sight of all their enemies shall they be glorified, and sit upon twelve thrones, (Matt. 19:28). And the upright shall have dominion over them in the morning, (Ps. 49:14), and shall, with Christ, judge the wicked, (I Cor. 6:2, 3). Then the wicked shall be cast into the fire that never shall be quenched, (Mark 9:46), into outer darkness, (Matt. 8:12). In the company of all devils, they shall blaspheme God day and night throughout an everlasting eternity, because of the pain.

Knowing the terror of the Lord, might we yet be persuaded to believe, and be provoked to jealousy of the eternal blessedness of God's people, that is despised and mocked in the world, but shall enter into eternal life.

This is the third benefit bequeathed unto God's Church in Christ. According to soul and body God's people shall ever be with the Lord, (I Thess. 4:17). They shall serve God without sin, without pain or sickness; they shall hunger no more, neither thirst any more; nor shall any harm befall them from the cold or heat, (Rev. 7:16, 17). With the innumerable multitudes of redeemed they shall everlastingly praise Him, Who sits upon the throne, and the Lamb, Who redeemed them to God by His blood, (Rev. 4:11; and Rev. 5:9, 12). And there shall be new heavens and a new earth, wherein dwelleth righteousness, and which the righteous shall inherit eternally.

That shall be the portion of God's elect. The Lord will wipe away tears from off all faces, and everlasting joy shall be upon their heads, (Isa. 25:8).

Happy is that people, whose God is the Lord. Of this Church of the Lord we must exclaim, as Moses did of Israel,

"Happy art thou, O Israel: who is like unto thee, O people saved by the Lord!"

PART VIII

Of the Profit of Faith, Being the Justification of the Sinner Before God

QUESTIONS 43-47

In this part of our exposition, the benefit of faith is spoken of.

As mentioned before, the Compendium speaks:

(a) Of the essence of faith, (Question 19);
(b) Of the sum of faith, (Questions 20-42);
(c) Of the profit of faith, (Questions 43-47);
(d) Of the Author of faith, (Question 48). — see Part IV.

The third of these is now to be dealt with, viz., The Profit of Faith. This profit is . . .

THE JUSTIFICATION OF THE SINNER BEFORE GOD

Only saving faith produces this profit. Neither historical, nor temporary, nor miraculous faith is able to justify us, because such a faith does not unite the sinner with Christ; and in Him alone can the hell-worthy sinner be absolved of guilt and punishment.

Therefore, when asked in . . . . .

Qu. 43: *What doth it profit thee now that thou believest all this?*

. . . the answer very properly states,

Answer: That I am righteous in Christ before God, Rom. 5:10.

. . . and . . .

Qu. 44: *How art thou righteous before God?*

Answer: Only by a true faith in Jesus Christ.

If we are destitute of *this* faith, we shall not be able to stand before God's judgment seat.

O, let each try himself whether he truly is implanted in Christ by faith; for he who is destitute of Him, is destitute of all good for eternity.

But is there then no justification before faith?

Yes, indeed. If there were no justification *before* faith, then justification *by* faith would not be possible.

Voetius says it so simply and plainly in his precious Catechism, where we read:

"Qu. *Does not justification precede faith?"*

"Ans. It can be said to precede, and also to follow."

"Qu. *How is it said to precede?"*

"Ans. Insomuch as it concerns a certain action or work of God, on and of His side alone."

"Qu. *How is justification said to be a fruit of faith and to follow in that order?"*

"Ans. Insomuch as it is wrought and received in us, applied to us, and terminates in us."

Would you be able to prove it also from Scripture that there is a justification prior to faith?

Yes; besides other places, this is taught in Rom. 4:25. Christ was raised for our justification. Christ was justified in His resurrection, and in Him his entire elect Church. The Apostle teaches this also in I Tim. 3:16, saying that Christ was justified in the Spirit.

JUSTIFICATION *before* faith is:

(a) From eternity, in the decrees of God; and,

(b) In the resurrection of Christ.

Thus Paul testifies in 2 Tim. 1:9, of the grace which is given unto the elect in Christ Jesus, before the world began.

But does not this justification, which is from eternity and in the resurrection of Christ, have to be applied in time?

Yes, indeed; for without the application of Christ and His righteousness, the elect also, like all men, are condemnable before God. Therefore justification by faith is indispensable to every man unto salvation. He who appeals unto the justification from eternity and in the resurrection of Christ, without being a partaker of justification by faith, deceives himself and denies the doctrine of Scripture, which tells us that the sinner is justified by or through faith.

We therefore maintain that there is a justification before faith, but also that justification by faith is indispensable.

This last puts us in a reconciled relation with God. For justification by faith is more than a becoming aware that we actually were justified already. O, it is something entirely different, for not one is righteous. An exchange of states takes place in justification by faith. In it the elect sinner leaves the state of condemnation, and enters into a state of reconciliation with God. He is absolved from guilt and punishment, and receives a claim to eternal life.

This is spoken of in the next question.

Qu. 45: *How is it to be understood that thou art justified by faith only?*

Answer: Thus: that the perfect satisfaction and righteousness of Christ alone are imputed to me of God, by which my sins are forgiven me, and I become an heir of everlasting life; and that I cannot receive that righteousness by any other means than by faith.

When speaking of justification, only one example is applicable, viz., that of the judge in the court of justice. For in justification, God, as judge, acquits the guilty sinner.

And how is this possible? God's justice must condemn the sinner to eternal death; and God cannot renounce His justice, or He would cease to be God. How then can He acquit a guilty sinner?

The sole ground of a sinner's justification before God is the righteousness of Christ, whereby satisfaction for all the sins of the elect is made, when justice avenged itself in the Surety. There is therefore but *one* ground for justification. That ground is the perfect satisfaction and righteousness of Christ. Anything outside of this is of no value. All our righteousnesses are as filthy rags; they cannot in the least, in whole or in part, satisfy the demands of God's justice. The satisfaction and righteousness of Christ are the sole ground upon which the elect sinner is justified.

But then they also must become ours.

And how do they become ours?

1. BY IMPUTATION;
2. BY RECEIVING.

In the acceptable time, God the Father imputes Christ and all His benefits unto the sinner, whom He justifies; and faith, which follows upon this imputation, appropriates Christ. The imputation precedes the receiving, but is also most certainly followed by it, so that there is no imputation without a receiving by faith.

However, there are steps in this receiving, and all the people of God do not arrive at the assurance of their justification in the court of their conscience.

In justification, two benefits are inseparably connected, viz.
1. The forgiveness of sins; and,
2. The title to eternal life.

We have already mentioned that but one example is applicable when speaking of justification, viz., that of the judge in the court of justice. The judge passes sentence; the advocate pleads; the sinner is summoned; Satan, the law, and one's own conscience accuse.

Now Christ, the Son of God, is the Advocate of Heaven, Who, on the ground of His satisfaction, demands acquittal. God the Father is judge, maintaining the injured justice of the Divine Essence. God the Spirit gives knowledge unto the sinner, and seals unto him his justification, applying Christ unto the heart. Thus each of the Divine Persons has His own economy, also in justification.

We must also observe that it is not the Advocate, but the Judge who acquits; not Christ, but the Father who justifies the sinner, and grants unto him the title of eternal life.

Blessed is the man unto whom the Lord imputeth not iniquity.

Christ, however, is the foundation upon which the sentence of the Father rests; He alone. Even faith, be it ever so valuable, does not furnish the least ground upon which we would be able to stand in the justice of God. As a ground, faith also falls away; it is Christ alone! Not a believer, but a hell-deserving sinner is justified, who, by virtue of his original and actual sins can await nothing but eternal death; and, O miracle of grace, he obtains eternal life.

Rome subverts the entire doctrine of justification. How could it be otherwise, while in heart and reins Rome hates free grace. They make good works their ground, and thus exclude grace, as spoken by Paul in Rom. 11:6, "And if by grace, then it is no more of works; otherwise grace is no more grace. But if it be of works, then it is no more grace: otherwise work is no more work."

Rome claims justification to be an outgrowth of sanctification, and confounds the one with the other. Although they are most intimately connected, yet they are distinct benefits.

What then is the difference between justification and sanctification?

Hellenbroek states very clearly:
1. Justification is an act without, but sanctification within us;
2. Justification removes the guilt, and sanctification the pollution of sin;
3. Sanctification is progressive here, but justification is perfect.

How is this to be understood? Does not justification by faith then take place within us? It is a subjective justification, is it not?

Yes, indeed! We have already stated that he, who does not learn to know this subjective justification, or, as Brakel calls it, effectual justification, lies under God's righteous judgment; is a child of wrath, and shall one day be condemned for eternity.

But when our old Divines spoke of justification, as being an act without us, they intended thereby that justification is a judicial act of God, decided without us in the tribunal of heaven, and proclaimed in the resurrection of Christ. Hereby the elect sinner, in the acceptable time, is translated into a reconciled state with God, and "effectually" acquitted. No inward change is wrought by justification, however, when it is taken by itself. The inward change comes with sanctification; this takes place within us.

With this the second point of difference between justification and sanctification is connected, viz., that justification removes the guilt of sin, and sanctification the pollution of sin.

Debts must be paid; pollution must be washed away. In justification there is a perfect satisfaction for all guilt of sin, to the very last farthing. Christ's righteousness is a complete and everlasting satisfaction for all the original and actual sins of His people. And upon this ground, the people of God are justified.

But justification does not wash away the pollution of sin.

The following example will make this clear:

There was a dock-hand, who shoveled coal throughout the entire day; he was as black as the coal itself. This man had a debt of $1000. He came on shore, and behold, there was a gentleman who gave him a receipt which showed that his debt was paid in full.

You can understand that this man leaped for joy. But, with all this, he remained as black as ever he was. To be delivered of this filth, he had to be washed.

Now in justification, the guilt of sin is removed, but not the filth of sin; God's people are cleansed of this in sanctification, which is inseparably connected with, yet is to be distinguished from justification.

The third point of difference is this: Sanctification is progressive here, justification is perfect.

A judge must either acquit or condemn a defendant; he cannot pass a partial judgment. In justification, God does not absolve His people in part, but gives them a complete acquittal.

But although sanctification is a renewing of the whole man, it is not perfect in this life. Perfect in the parts, but incomplete in the degrees. God's people have a law in their members, warring against the law of their mind, and bringing them into captivity to the law of sin. In heaven, sanctification shall be completed in glorification.

Thus justification and sanctification are distinguished.

Rome, however, is a stranger to, and an enemy of Scriptural justification. It seeks to be justified by works; but, as the instructor teaches in the next question, this is impossible.

Qu. 46: *Why cannot our good works be our righteousness before God, or some part thereof?*

Answer: Because even our best works, in this life, are imperfect, and polluted with sins.

By the deeds of the law there shall no flesh be justified before God, (Rom. 3:20). By grace are ye saved through faith; and that not of yourselves; it is the gift of God: Not of works, lest any man should boast, (Eph. 2:8, 9).

Thus God's Word severs all works in regard to justification. How does Rome venture to say even one word in favor of it?

But they have a subterfuge: Does not God reward good works? Yes, indeed; not only in this, but also in the life to come.

Where do you read of such a rewarding? In Psalm 19:11, "In keeping of God's law there is great reward." And in Rev. 14:13, "Blessed are the dead which die in the Lord, . . .their works do follow them." Surely will God reward good works.

Qu. 47: *Do our good works then merit nothing, which yet God will reward in this, and in a future life?*

Answer: This reward is not given out of merit, but of grace.

The Lord Jesus Himself gave an evident example of this in the parable of the laborers in the vineyard.

The first group of laborers, whom the owner of the vineyard hired, had agreed to work for a stipulated wage, a penny a day. They received the wages they earned.

But the laborers which followed, also received a penny, but this was not merited; they received a reward of mercy.

And now the Lord rewards the works of His people with the entire exclusion of merit; all, *absolutely all*, is grace. The people of God are not justified by works, but by grace. For that people, therefore, there remains but one ground upon which they shall glory, viz., Christ, Who by grace, is given unto them. Thus they are justified by faith, and have peace with God through our Lord Jesus Christ, (Rom. 5:1).

Shall it be well with us, we must learn to know something of this justification.

One day the Lord shall present those who are justified by faith, righteous upon the clouds, when He comes to judge the quick and the dead; and they shall enter into eternal life.

We therefore can consider justification to be as follows:

A. PRECEDING FAITH, namely,
1. from eternity; and,
2. in the resurrection of Christ.

B. BY FAITH, namely,
1. in the exchange of states in regeneration; and,
2. in the court of the conscience.

C. ONE TIME UPON THE CLOUDS OF HEAVEN.

Of the Means of Grace

QUESTIONS 48-52

With this part of our exposition of The Compendium, we have arrived at the last of the four points dealing with faith, viz., of

THE AUTHOR OF FAITH

This Author is the Spirit. In Part IV, the Essence of Faith was spoken of: and mention was made also of historical, temporal and miraculous faith. Now we are to speak of the Author of faith.

Qu. 48: *Who worketh that faith in thee?*

Answer: The Holy Ghost.

We therefore do not have that true upright faith of ourselves. No man can say that Jesus is the Lord, but by the Holy Ghost, (I Cor. 12:3). Faith is the gift of God, (Eph. 2:8). That faith is wrought by the Spirit in God's elect. All have not this faith; it is the "faith of God's elect," (Titus 1:1): it is "the faith of the operation of God." (Col. 2:12). Although we believe Scripture, as is written of Agrippa, yet we are not the possessors of true faith, unless we are regenerated.

In regeneration, God the Holy Ghost infuses faith into the soul, as a living plant. This plant never dies. Although the exercise of faith is often very weak, and unbelief on the other hand powerful, yet God's people can never again lose saving faith. That faith is of God. The Spirit is the Author of it.

Furthermore, the Lord works that faith by *means,* as we hear in the following question.

Qu. 49: *By what means?*

Answer: By the hearing of the Word preached, Rom. 10:14-17.

Thus the Lord Himself devised the means to work faith in the hearts of His people. The means to this end is the preached Word. God's Word speaks of it, for instance, in Rom. 10:17, "So then faith cometh by hearing, and hearing by the Word of God." Lydia is likewise an evidence of it, that faith is wrought by means of the preached Word. The Lord opened her heart under Paul's preaching, that she attended unto the things which were spoken of him.

By this appointment of God it is evident how dreadful it is to slight and neglect the preaching of God's Word. Especially in these days of profound declension do many turn away from the church and seek their delight in worldly pleasures.

O, girls and boys, never neglect the ministration of God's Word; do not absent yourself from church; neither at the morning, afternoon nor evening services. Those empty places shall one day testify against us. Then we shall cry out: "O, that I had betaken myself to the preaching of God's Word; it might have been the means to my conversion." God is pleased to work faith through these means.

Not all, however, who hear the preached Word, receive this saving faith. There is an external and an internal calling.

The external call comes to all who hear the Word preached. It calls to conversion; it invites to salvation; it proffers Christ to lost sinners. By this external call God Himself invites the sinner, and sends His ambassadors who, with holy zeal and faithfulness, as though God did beseech the sinner by them, entreat them in Christ's stead: "Be ye reconciled to God," (2 Cor. 5:20). The external call is not to be lightly esteemed; it is God's message to us. That it bears no fruit to salvation, is not the fault of the Gospel, nor of God Who calls by means of the Gospel, and even confers various gifts unto those whom He calls; but the fault lies in those who are called. Read attentively Art. 9 and 10 of the Third and Fourth Heads of Doctrine of our Canons of Dort. It shall be our own fault if the Word is not instrumental to our conversion.

Yet the external call is not saving. If faith is to be wrought by the Word, then the Spirit must fructify it.

But now the question arises: How can God's proffer of salvation be well-intended when it is made even to reprobates, of whom

He had determined in His eternal counsel that they should not obtain salvation?

It can be so only because God's glory stands above our salvation. The Lord seeks His own glory, also by the preaching of the Word. He shall be glorified in those who are lost, as well as in those who are saved; as Paul says in 2 Cor. 2:15, 16, "For we are unto God a sweet savor of Christ, in them that are saved, and in them that perish: To the one we are the savor of death unto death; and to the other the savor of life unto life."

Now the Lord has in view the glory of His attributes in proffering salvation to all those unto whom He sends His Word and whom He invites and calls. His proffer is true, and it shall redound to the glory of His justice, as well as of His mercy. For none shall be able to give any blame unto God, should he perish under the hearing of the Word; that is solely the fruit of the hardness and obduracy of his heart.

Nevertheless, the internal call is indispensable, if the Word shall bear fruit and faith shall be wrought thereby. The external persuasion has no power to break our hard and stony hearts. God the Spirit alone is able to do this. He accompanies the preached Word, and gives it entrance into the soul, renewing and breaking it. The Spirit worketh faith: the preached Word is but the means appointed by Him.

May it serve us to that end; how great would be that privilege.

This wrought faith stands continually in need of being strengthened. The Spirit also works this strengthening by means. To accomplish this, He uses the same preached Word and the Sacraments.

Qu. 50: *How does He strengthen that faith?*

Answer: By the same Word preached, and by the use of the holy sacraments.

The Word, thus, has a double operation; it serves to work faith and to strengthen faith. But the sacraments are means only to strengthen faith. One unconverted may not, therefore, make use of the sacraments to obtain faith: the preaching of the Word, (as the means), serves for that purpose. Through these means the Lord is also pleased to sustain the life in His people. He blesses the preaching, that His people may grow in faith. Thus the ministration of God's Word remains precious unto His people, and a day in His courts is better than a thousand.

It is indeed a discouraging sign when God's children no longer seek the preaching of the Word, and think they can live well enough without it.

The sacraments also serve to strengthen the faith wrought within us.

It is the sacraments of which we are now to speak.

Qu. 51: *What are the sacraments?*

Answer: They are holy signs and seals instituted by God, thereby to assure us, that He of grace grants us remission of sins, and life eternal, for the sake of that one sacrifice of Christ finished on the cross.

In this question, and the next, the following things are spoken of:

(a) The NAME;
(b) The ESSENCE;
(c) The PURPOSE;
(d) The NUMBER of the sacraments.

(a) THE NAME

The word sacrament does not appear in the Bible. Rome however says that it does, and quotes Eph. 5:32; but the word sacrament is not found there, but the phrase, "This is a great mystery." But not every mystery is a sacrament. But Rome wants it to mean sacrament, so that by this distorting of Scripture they elevate marriage, to include it with the sacraments.

Luther, and others, raised objections to the word sacrament, but although this name does not occur in the Bible, it nevertheless is permissible for us to use it, as well as, for instance, the word "trinity." In the Latin original it is very evident what we are to understand by sacraments, viz., the signs and seals instituted of God.

In Holy Scripture, the sacraments are therefore called: signs, seals, covenants and tokens of the covenant. (See Romans 4:11; Gen. 17:11, 13; Exodus 12:13.

(b) THE ESSENCE

"Sacraments are holy signs and seals instituted by God," says the instructor.

In the first place, sacraments are signs. Rome emphasizes action in the sacrament, and sees in it a function of the church, to dispense grace. The Reformers, however, basing their decision on God's Word, resolutely emphasized that sacraments are signs; without signs, no sacraments.

These signs are: water, pure water, in Holy Baptism; and common, nourishing bread and wine, in the Lord's Supper.

These signs are holy, because He Who instituted the sacraments is holy. They were instituted by God; and the signifying tokens employed therein and the users and use thereof, are likewise holy.

Sacraments, however, are not only mere signs; they are also seals. Abraham received the sign of circumcision unto a seal of the righteousness of faith, (Rom. 4:11).

Some regarded the sacraments as no more than mere signs. And who were these?

Zwingli, and the Remonstrants who followed him in this error; and also many Mennonites. It is an old Socinian error, contrary to that which is clearly proclaimed in God's Word, and therefore contrary to the essence of the sacraments. Sacraments are signs and seals.

(c) THE PURPOSE

In Qu. 51, this purpose is described thus: "thereby to assure us, that He of grace grants us remission of sins and life eternal, for the sake of that one sacrifice of Christ, finished on the cross."

The Lord therefore is pleased to assure us of remission of sins through the use of the sacraments. This assurance is God's work. Not every one that is baptized: not every communicant, receives this assurance. The one sacrifice of Christ has been finished on the cross for His elect. Unto them grace is given, and the Lord is pleased also to assure them of this grace.

From this we also observe that God's people do not first have to be assured of grace before they may partake of communion, for this is exactly the way in which the Lord is pleased to work assurance, viz., by the use thereof, that His people may be given to cry out with Job, "I have heard of Thee by the hearing of the ear, but now mine eye seeth Thee." For in the sacraments, the Lord, as it were, gives His favored people to see who He is for them and what He acquired for them. The sacraments are therefore visible signs and seals.

May God's children increasingly make a faithful improvement thereof.

(d) THE NUMBER

This is spoken of in the next question.

Qu. 52: *How many sacraments hath Christ instituted in the New Testament?*

Answer: Two: Holy Baptism, and the Holy Supper.

To these two Rome has added five spurious sacraments; for the laity, for instance, they have marriage, which they forbid the clergy. Rome also made sacraments which are only for the clergy, and in which those poor creatures, the laity, must have no part, as for instance, ordination.

What then are these seven Romish sacraments?

They are, besides baptism and the Lord's Supper, confirmation, penance, marriage, ordination, and extreme unction.

These are nothing but popish inventions contrary to God's Word. This Word speaks of only two sacraments of the New Covenant: Holy Baptism and the Holy Supper.

In the Old Testment dispensation there likewise were two sacraments, viz., Circumcision and the Passover. Extraordinary sacraments are spoken of, as: Noah's ark, of which baptism is the antitype, (I Pet. 3:21) ; the Red Sea; the pillar of a cloud; the Rock; which all pointed to Christ, (I Cor. 10:1-4).

But the Lord instituted circumcision and the passover as sacraments for the people of the Old Covenant.

Was there any distinction between the sacraments of the Old and of the New Testament?

YES.

(a) Those of the Old Covenant were bloody;
Those of the New Testament were not bloody.

(b) The sacraments of the Old Testament pointed to Christ *as to come;* while those of the New Testament to Christ *as already come,* and as having completed His Mediatorial work on earth.

Circumcision and Passover were actually sacraments, signs and seals instituted by God, unto assurance of the grace in Christ.

Rome, and also Luther, deny this. They cannot reconcile their transubstantiation and consubstantiation with the Old Covenant. In order to teach these erroneous doctrines, it was first necessasary for Christ to have been on earth. But God's Word refutes this, and makes special mention of the institution of:

(a)   Circumcision, in Genesis 17; and,

(b)   The Passover, in Exodus 12.

But did the Covenant of Works also have sacraments?

Not as signs and seals of the forgiveness of sins; that could not be, because there was no sin while the Covenant of Works was in effect.

Some of our Reformed theologians, however, call the tree of life a sacrament, but that can be accepted only in this sense, that this tree sealed the promise of life upon obedience.

In the Covenant of Works, however, there was no occasion for a sacrament that assured of the forgiveness of sin by virtue of the one only sacrifice of Christ. The sacraments belong to the Covenant of Grace.

Then the rainbow, in a relative sense, can also be called a sacrament. The covenant with Noah did not imply the forgiveness of sins for Christ's sake; but only temporal promises made unto all mankind, yea, unto the beasts of the field and the grass of the earth, viz., that God would not again destroy the earth by water. The rainbow assures us of these promises, but it is not a sacrament of the grace of the elect in Christ.

The Lord does take the oath, sworn in His covenant with Noah, as an example of His faithfulness unto His people, saying, "As I have sworn that the waters of Noah should no more go over the earth; so have I sworn that I would not be wroth with thee, nor rebuke thee," (Isa. 54:9). And the Lord swears this oath in the sacraments of Baptism and the Lord's Supper.

Happy is that people, that may experience the power thereof.

We hope to speak of Holy Baptism in the following lesson.

Of Holy Baptism

QUESTIONS 53-56

In the preceding lesson we have spoken of the sacraments in general, as they are signs and seals of the forgiveness of sins for the sake of Christ's blood.

We now enter into a discussion of each of these two sacraments of the New Testament in particular; first of *Holy Baptism*, and then of the *Holy Supper*.

The Compendium devotes four questions to Holy Baptism, Questions 53 - 56.

Qu. 53: *Which is the outward sign in Baptism?*

Answer: The water, with which we are baptized in the name of the Father, and of the Son, and of the Holy Ghost.

We already have mentioned that in baptism, common, unmixed water must be used. Rome uses water that is consecrated by the priest.

What does the use of water signify?

The water represents the cleansing by Christ's blood, and therefore it must be nothing but common, pure water. It is with this that we cleanse our body, and in baptism it signifies the blood of Christ that cleanses from sin.

In this manner did John baptize in Jordan, and thus also was the eunuch baptized in the water, which was along the way that goes down unto Gaza, (Acts 8:36-39). No Romish consecration was of any use here whatever.

In baptism, the water is administered either by immersion or by sprinkling. The signification of either method is identical. In the Old Testament, therefore, sprinkling was used as well as immersion in the ceremonial cleansing. Moses sprinkled the blood of the covenant upon the people, (Ex. 24:8). In Ezek. 36:25, the Lord says, "I will sprinkle clean water upon you;" and Paul speaks in Heb. 12:24, of "the blood of sprinkling."

The position taken by the Baptists and Mormons that baptism may be administered by immersion only, is therefore untenable. They distinguish themselves by their foolish insistence on this point, whereby each may the easier guard himself against their false doctrines.

In sprinkling and immersion is found the same underlying signification.

Baptism may be administered only once, as this is the sacrament of birth, the same as the Holy Supper is the sacrament of continual strengthening. The Reformers were therefore very cautious to guard against a multiple administration of baptism. They, for instance, refrained from baptizing a second time, any who had been baptized by Rome. The Church of God was included in that of Rome during the Middle Ages. The Reformers would have disregarded this fact, if they had administered baptism unto those delivered from Romish idolatry.

Our Reformed fathers, however, refused to acknowledge the Romish baptism of extremity, administered by those who were not church officers. *That* was not a baptism.

For a formal acknowledgement of baptism, these two things are required:

1. That baptism is performed in the name of the Father, and of the Son, and of the Holy Ghost; and,

2. That baptism is administered by one who is a regularly constituted office-bearer in any particular circle.

We are directed to this in the answer given to Question 53. No one may officiate in the name of the Triune God who is not in office. Therefore the Romish baptism of extremity, whether performed by doctor, midwife, nurse , or whoever it may be, is a mockery. No Protestant is permitted to administer such a baptism. Our doctors and nurses must steadfastly refuse to baptize. Should they perform any act, like baptism, in the name of Father, Son and Holy Ghost, they would make themselves guilty of profaning God's majesty.

But where does Rome ever get that so-called "baptism of extremity?"

It flows from this, that Rome makes salvation dependent upon baptism. Fellowship with God is restored by baptism, they say. Therefore baptism is urged at all costs, that no child die unbaptized; so anyone may baptize in an extremity, whether neighbor or policeman, it makes no difference whatever.

What blindness! God does not make His grace dependent upon a sacrament; and no one may baptize who is not lawfully authorized thereto, for he, who baptizes, must officiate in the name of the Father, and the Son, and the Holy Ghost.

Now the Compendium asks concerning the signification of Baptism.

Qu. 54: *What doth that signify and seal?*

Answer: The washing away of sins by the blood and Spirit of Jesus Christ.

Thus baptism, with common, pure water, in the name of the Triune God, signifies and seals two benefits, namely, justification and sanctification: for thereby alone does the cleansing of sin take place. And this cleansing is accomplished by the blood of Christ, (I John 1:7). Water cannot wash away sin, but it signifies and seals the cleansing by the blood of Christ, *for all the elect, and for them only.*

But why then does Ananias say to Paul, "Be baptized and wash away thy sins," (Acts 22:16), and how then can baptism, in Titus 3:5, be called, "the washing of regeneration," if the water does not cleanse and regenerate?

That is very simple, because the places mentioned speak not only of the sign, but of the thing signified; not of the water, but of the baptism of the Spirit, which regenerates and assures of the cleansing of sin by the blood of Christ.

Water baptism is a sign and seal: neither less, nor more. The Council of Trent erred most dreadfully therefore when they determined that water baptism washed away original sin, and is indispensable unto salvation. That is contrary to I John 1:7.

Moreover, all who are baptized do not receive the grace that is signified and sealed in baptism. Ishmael and Esau received the sacrament, and were lost; also Judas and Simon the Sorcerer furnish proof that the sacrament does not impart salvation.

Abraham, the Eunuch, Cornelius, Paul and the Jailer already had the grace imparted unto them, that is sealed in the sacrament, before they received the sacrament. It therefore was not imparted unto them in baptism.

Unbaptized, the thief on the cross entered into heaven. Not the water in baptism, but the blood of Jesus Christ cleanseth from sin, (I Cor. 6:11; Heb. 9:14; I John 1:7). This grace is signified and sealed in baptism.

Therefore it is not sufficient for us to be baptized. We must be regenerated. O, how sadly dissappointed shall all be, even those of a Reformed confession, who boast of their water-baptism, but have never obtained fellowship with Christ.

It should be the primary concern of each of us to become implanted in Christ by faith.

For them, who are implanted in Christ by faith, *and for them only,* does baptism assure of the washing away of sin.

The form of Baptism speaks explicitly of this.

In baptism, God the Father witnesses and seals unto us, that He does make an eternal covenant of grace with us, adopts us for His children and heirs, and therefore will provide us with every good thing and avert all evil or turn it to our profit.

With whom does God the Father establish the Covenant of Grace? Whom does He adopt to be His children? And for whom shall all things work together for good? Does this concern all who are baptized? Indeed not; but it applies to God's elect. The Father seals it unto them.

In like manner the Son in baptism seals unto us that He does wash us in His blood from all our sins. That is not merely an external matter, but is that perfect redemption and cleansing, in the fellowship of His death and resurrection, unto the salvation of our souls. It is the sealing of the elect.

And the Holy Ghost assures their being brought unto salvation, at such a time as has been determined in the eternal counsel of God.

This assurance of the Holy Spirit is not something that is dependent upon the conduct of man, as if God would have to await our willingness. For of ourselves we would never be willing to be saved by grace.

When the Holy Spirit assures us that He will dwell in us, and sanctify us to be members of Christ (as it is written in the Form for the Administration of Baptism), then that is the assurance of His sovereign will, which shall surely be performed out of free grace in all those purchased with Christ's blood, and unto whom the purchased redemption shall be applied. They shall furthermore be kept by the power of God, through faith, unto salvation ready to be revealed in the last time, (I Peter 1:5). To that end the Holy Spirit shall apply unto them that, which they already possess *in Christ;* in Him, Who is glorified at the right hand of the Father. In Him all the elect already possess that perfect salvation: and they alone.

The Holy Spirit shall moreover:

1. Impute unto them the benefits which they have in Christ;
2. Renew them daily, till they shall finally be presented without spot or wrinkle among the assembly of the elect in eternal life.

How evident should it then be to all, that, in baptism, not merely outward benefits are assured unto all that are baptized. Whosoever teaches this, makes Holy Baptism of none effect. But, in baptism, the Triune God seals eternal salvation unto all whom He has chosen and purchased with His blood, and whom He himself shall make partakers of this salvation, through the washing away of sin by the blood of Christ. The promises of the Gospel are sealed in Baptism, as shown in the next question.

Qu. 55: *Where hath Christ promised and assured us of this?*

Answer: In the institution of baptism; which is as follows: "Go ye into all the world, and preach the gospel to every creature. He that believeth and is baptized shall be saved, but he that believeth not, shall be damned." (Mark 16:15, 16).

Here the Lord states incontrovertibly that whosoever is void of true faith, although he is baptized, shall be damned.

But does not this text imply that man first must believe, and then be baptized, and that children therefore may not be baptized?

Indeed Not! Listen to the instructor in ...

Qu. 56: *Are infants also to be baptized?*

Answer: Yes, for they, as well as the adult, are comprehended
        in the covenant of God, and in his church.

We are now to deal with:

INFANT BAPTISM

Relating to this, we propose three questions:

A. Shall infants be baptized?

B. On what grounds shall infants be baptized?

C. Which infants shall be baptized?

A. SHALL INFANTS BE BAPTIZED?

To this question, there are those who would answer: *No.* They
are the Anabaptists, and the Baptists. They say:

1. Nowhere are we commanded to baptize infants; and,

2. They base their assertion on Mark 16:16.

In this however, they err.

1. A separate injunction for infant baptism was not necessary.
It was at God's command that children received the sacrament of
circumcision. Baptism is come in place of circumcision, (Colossians 2:11, 12). Now if children were not to be baptized, the
Lord would have forbidden it explicitly; but this He did not do.
Consequently the sacrament must be administered unto infants;
they must be baptized.

2. Mark 16:16 does not say: You must wait with baptizing
any until he shall have made confession of faith, but that salvation
and faith are joined together.

Moreover, the command given in Mark 16:16 refers to the
mission work of the apostles. And missionaries do not begin by
baptizing the children of the heathens, but, when these are brought
unto faith, they and their children are baptized.

In this Baptists err; they sever the church of the New Testament
from that of the old covenant. Children must be baptized.

B. ON WHAT GROUND SHALL INFANTS BE BAPTIZED

The Compendium states: "They, as well as the adult are comprehended in the covenant of God, and in His Church." That is the
ground for infant baptism.

But how must this be understood? Do not only the elect belong to the Covenant of Grace?

Yes, only the elect. For them Christ suffered, and for them He is glorified. *They* are set with Him in heaven; in Him *they* are partakers of salvation, and *they* shall be washed in Christ's blood. It is therefore by means of this holy sacrament that the Holy Spirit assures *the elect* that He will dwell in them and sanctify them to be members of Christ, applying unto them that which they have in Christ, namely, the washing away of their sins and the daily renewing of their lives, till they shall finally be presented without spot among the assembly of the elect in life eternal.

How clearly and incontrovertibly does the Form for the Administration of Baptism teach in these words that the sealing in baptism concerns *the elect,* and not all who are baptized. The elect, and not all of mankind, are included in the Covenant of Grace in Christ, their Head, and, in Him, are partakers of the benefits of the covenant, which are applied unto them in the time of God's good pleasure. This is assured unto them in baptism. And, since God has His elect among children, as well as among adults, Holy Baptism must be administered also unto them.

But, as we already observed in Part I, there is also an external revelation of the Covenant of Grace, which comprehends many who shall not receive salvation, and are thus never incorporated into the covenant. Still they live within the confines of the covenant revelation, and stand to a certain degree in an external relation of this covenant. Their congregation is holy, the same as that of Israel in the Old Testament was holy, although not every Israelite was sanctified in the blood of Christ.

Regarding this external relation, they are all comprehended in the covenant and the church. Baptism therefore appertains also unto them, in contradistinction to the children of the heathen, as we shall consider shortly.

The promise, however, is only unto the elect; unto them, children as well as adults, is salvation promised, and grace in Christ is sealed in baptism unto them only.

But are we then to presume that all children presented for baptism are elect and regenerated?

Dr. A. Kuyper strongly insisted on this, and even ejects out of The Christian Reformed Church any who does not presume this, (E. Voto II, 54). He further writes that the church "is to suppose the newly-born to be already regenerated, and is to baptize them on this ground."

But we reject this doctrine, because:

(a) A presupposition *can never serve as a basis for baptism;* infant baptism has a firmer foundation than presumptive regeneration, namely, the immovable covenant, and the infallible promises of God. And,

(b) The grace which is sealed in baptism is *not a subjective,* but an *objective grace in Christ.* The question is not whether these parents, or these infants are regenerated or not regenerated, that grace may be assured in their hearts; but, in baptism, God confirms His Covenant unto the salvation of His elect, and to the comfort of all His people; (Read Comrie, Examination of Tolerance, II, 283; IV, 493).

In due season God shall apply unto His elect and purchased with Christ's blood, the benefits of the Covenant: the one in his youth, the other in a more advanced age, according to His sovereign good pleasure. This God seals in baptism. There is nothing for us to presume in baptism.

But are we not taught in the Canons of Dort that all children who die in infancy, go to heaven?

The Canons of Dort, First Head of Doctrine, Art. 17, declare: "Since we are to judge of the will of God from His Word, which testifies that the children of believers are holy, not by nature, but in virtue of the covenant of grace, in which they, together with the parents, are comprehended, godly parents have no reason to doubt of the election and salvation of their children, whom it pleaseth God to call out of this life in their infancy."

This article by no means implies, however, that each and every child shall go to heaven if he dies in his infancy. The church fathers of Dort never did affirm this.

That is clearly manifested by the Acts of the Synod of Dort, as, for instance, the judgment given by the delegates of Utrecht.

They said:

"For salvation, and the promise thereof, emanate solely from election unto salvation. Now the promise is unto young children: I am thy God and the God of thy seed. Your children are holy: and the promise of salvation is unto them: Let them come unto Me, for of such is the kingdom of heaven.

If election, then, applies unto young children, so likewise does reprobation apply to them. Such was manifested by the rejection of Esau, being yet a young child; yea, being not yet born. Which example the Apostle advances to manifest conclusively the general doctrine of reprobation, drawing his inferences from a particular instance as evidence of the truth of it in general, the same as the Apostle confirms the doctrine of the election of God, with the example of Jacob, being yet an infant: as yet unborn."

Thus it is evident that the Canons of Dort do not teach that *all* children who die in their infancy are chosen and consequently go to heaven. Among them some are chosen; others rejected.

Why then do the divines of Dort speak in such a manner?

They did this to defend themselves against the slander of the Remonstrants. The Remonstrants deny God's sovereign election. They wanted an election founded on foreseen faith and good works. And whereas infants can neither exercise faith nor perform good works, the Arminians slandered those of the Reformed faith by saying that they in fact *condemned* young children.

It was to counteract this calumny that the divines at Dort spoke in the manner they did, when composing the Canons.

God has His elect also among children who die in their infancy, and shall receive them in glory, as is evident with the child of David, and also that of Jeroboam. Of the certainty of this none have to doubt. But that does not imply that *all* children that die in their infancy shall be saved. Only they who belong to the Covenant of Grace shall be saved. They are chosen unto salvation in Christ.

Would not the children be chosen in their parents, and in them have a title to salvation, as long as they have not yet attained unto the age of discretion?

Indeed not! How does anyone ever arrive at such an unscriptural thesis. It is to be wholly rejected, for:

(a) Election did not take place in the parents, but in Christ, (Eph. 1:4);

(b) God's counsel in immutable.

How could children (included in their parents) be partakers of salvation, only to lose the same again when coming to years of discretion? What kind of doctrine would that be?

There is no apostacy of the saints.

But does not baptism serve to strengthen faith? And in order to strengthen faith, it must necessarily be there.

Most assuredly; but that does not mean to say that faith in a baptized child in strengthened, for,

(1) Even though a child presented for baptism had faith, it still cannot be mediately strengthened by the sacrament, seeing that a strengthening by means can take place only in respect to the exercise of faith; and an infant cannot exercise faith, no more than it can think, although born with an understanding.

(2) It is not the faith of the child which is strengthened by baptism, but the faith of the people of God who obtained salvation in the blood of Christ.

Thus infant baptism does not have a subjective ground, but objective, namely, the ground of God's covenant and promises. In baptism, the Lord assures salvation unto His people; and this sealing is for strengthening them, who believe Him in truth.

C. WHICH CHILDREN SHALL BE BAPTIZED?

Only those children who are born in the church; who outwardly are included in the covenant. No children, therefore, of heathens, Mohammedans and Jews. The administration of Holy Baptism is limited to the confines of the church, just as circumcision in olden times was limited to Israel. But unto those children, however, the sign and seal of Holy Baptism *must* be administered. Baptism is essential, not in that it can impart salvation, but *by virtue of Christ's command.*

How lamentable it is that many, in a Christian country, are unbaptized and revert to heathenism. Let us not despise God's covenant. Many are inclined to consider baptism a mere formality, which has no connection whatever with salvation.

To refute Rome's error, we insist that baptism does not impart salvation; nevertheless, we must submit ourselves to the Lord's command, and not withhold our children from baptism. The Lord's displeasure shall rest upon this negligence. It shall one day be revealed, when we and our seed shall stand before God's tribunal.

If there ever was a need to give serious consideration to God's ordinances, then it is certainly in these days of deep declension, and of increasing paganism. Children must be baptized.

We are not however, to make baptism the ground of our salvation. Many who are baptized, are strangers to a work of grace.

O, that our ear would be unstopped for God's promises, and our eye opened for the sealing thereof in baptism, so that we would learn to seek the Lord, and that one day our baptized forehead shall not witness against us in the day of days.

PART X

Of the Lord's Supper

QUESTIONS 57-63

The Holy Supper is called the Lord's Supper in I Cor. 11:20. Besides this name, Scripture speaks of: the Lord's table, I Cor. 10:21; the breaking of bread, Acts 2:42; the communion of the body and blood of Christ, I Cor. 10:16.

Of the Lord's Supper, it must likewise be said that it is a sign and a seal. The material elements which Christ ordained for the keeping of the Lord's Supper are bread and wine; as seen in. .

Qu. 57: *What is the outward sign in the Lord's Supper?*

Answer: The broken bread that we eat, and the poured out wine which we drink, in remembrance of the sufferings and death of Christ.

Thus there cannot be solely a spiritual keeping of this sacrament. Although there is a spiritual fellowship with Christ, other than at the communion table, this by no means gives liberty to neglect Christ's commandment of love. The Lord Jesus, the same night in which He was betrayed, said, "This do in remembrance of me," (Luke 22:19), and this should exercise such an influence in the soul of God's children, that not one of them could refrain from showing His death. Alas! how sad it is in this respect with many.

The visible signs used in the Lord's Supper are common and nourishing bread and wine. The bread is to be broken, to signify the breaking of Christ's body; and the wine is to be poured out, to signify the shedding of Christ's blood. By the use of these signs the Lord wants to assure His people that He feeds and nourishes their souls to everlasting life.

Qu. 58: *What is thereby signified and sealed?*

Answer: That Christ, with His crucified body and shed blood, feeds and nourishes our souls to everlasting life.

Thus it is not the bread and wine that feeds and nourishes the soul of God's children: no more than the visible sign of water in baptism can wash away sins. But the signs in the Lord's Supper direct us to Christ, and the Lord is pleased, by the eating of the bread and the drinking of the wine, to strengthen the faith of His people; to cause them to look upon that one only sacrifice which was offered on the cross: to apply the same unto the forgiveness of sins and a closer union with Him, so that the Lord's people may walk in communion with Him as flesh of His flesh and bone of His bones.

The Lord Himself promised that He would strengthen faith by the keeping of the Supper, as we see in . . .

Qu. 59: Where hath Christ promised such things to us?

Answer: In the institution of the Lord's Supper, which is thus expressed, by Paul, in I Cor. 11:23, 24, 25, 26:

> "For I have received of the Lord, that which also I delivered unto you, that the Lord Jesus the same night in which he was betrayed, took bread; and when he had given thanks, brake it, and said, Take, eat; this is my body, which is broken for you; this do in remembrance of me. After the same manner also He took the cup, when He had supped, saying, This cup is the new testament in my blood: this do ye, as oft as ye drink it, in remembrance of me. For as often as ye eat this bread, and drink this cup, ye do show the Lord's death till He come."

The Lord's Supper, therefore, is not a human institution; the Lord Himself ordained the Supper. Paul emphasizes this fact in I Cor. 10:16, 17; 11:24, 25. And this statute of the Lord is appointed for all ages, until He comes on the clouds of heaven. However dark the times may become, this ordinance of Christ continues in effect for all who fear Him. They have to partake of the Supper; to eat the bread and drink the wine where the congregation assembles. For it is only in this assembly that the Lord's Supper may be administered. And inasmuch as the Lord's table shall be prepared till the day of His coming, so likewise shall the visible church be in existence until the end of days. God's people are in need of spiritual nourishment, even as our bodies need meat; and the Lord is pleased to give this spiritual nourishment mediately in the partaking of the Lord's Supper. Neglecting this sacrament therefore causes the life of God's people to languish, although it remains sure, that only bread and wine are partaken of with the natural mouth; for these symbols remain what they are.

Qu. 60: *Is the bread changed into the body of Christ, and the wine into His blood?*

Answer: No; no more than the water in baptism is changed into the blood of Christ.

In regard to the doctrine of the Lord's Supper, there are two gross errors especially that we have to contend with, namely, that of consubstantiation and transubstantiation.

By consubstantiation we refer to the error of Luther. Consubstantiation means coexistence, and therefore shows that Luther taught that Christ is present in the Lords' Supper not only with His Godhead, majesty, grace and Spirit, but also with His human nature; present at, with, and in the symbols of bread and wine. This is in closest conformity with the doctrine also taught by Luther, concerning Christ's omnipresence according to His human nature, as spoken of when discoursing upon Christ's ascension. And, having once deviated to the inconceivable fallacy that the Divine attribute of omnipresence was transferred, in the ascension, to Christ's human nature, Luther taught that Christ is present with His human nature also at, with, and in the symbols of bread and wine in the Lord's Supper. Although he alienated himself from the doctrines of Rome, which hold that the substance of bread and wine are changed into the body and blood of Christ, yet Luther erred greatly.

According to His human nature, Christ is in heaven: but according to His Godhead, He is everywhere present. And as such He is not *in* the symbols, but is *present at* the Lord's Supper, and that according to His Godhead and Spirit only, to strengthen His people by means of these signs.

More abominable still is Rome's doctrine of *transubstantiation.*

Transubstantiation means transformation. Rome asserts that at the very pronouncing of the sacramental words of consecration by the priest, the bread and wine are transformed into the body and blood of Christ; yea, into the Mediator Himself. Then bread is no longer bread, and then wine is no longer wine; but it is then the Lord Jesus Himself. Then also, when the Papist partakes of communion, he does not eat a morsel of bread with his natural mouth, but Christ Himself. It then would be sacrilege indeed, if, in the breaking of the bread or in the drinking of the wine, one crumb or one drop were lost. To prevent this, Rome bakes wafers, also called the host, and for the same reason the cup does not pass from mouth to mouth, but the priest drinks the wine for all communicants.

How it is possible that even one person can believe such lying doctrines is almost inconceivable. For Rome's transubstantiation is so palpable a falsehood, that even the blind can feel it. Did then a transformation take place from bread and wine into flesh and blood? Then we would be able to notice it. When God turned all the waters of Egypt into blood, the fish died and the waters stank: for these waters were truly changed; every Egyptian perceived it. And when the Lord Jesus changed water into wine at the marriage at Cana in Galilee, it was to be seen and tasted. But the Romish wafer remains a wafer still. Behold it: taste it: let it be chemically analyzed, and the answer, without exception, will be, it is not flesh: it is bread. The same is true of the wine. Therefore, this transubstantiation is a lie.

But there is more. Transubstantiation is an accursed idolatry. Rome demands the host, this consecrated wafer, to be worshipped. For, say they, this has now become Christ Himself, both according to His Divine and human nature. Rome therefore requires that Divine adoration be shown unto this baked wafer.

And, thirdly, from Rome's transubstantiation originated the absurd doctrine of the sacrifice of the mass. The mass is not to be confused with the Lord's Supper: it is supposed to signify a sacrifice. That the Lord Jesus died once on the cross is not enough for Rome; no, He must yet die daily at the hands of the priests, and that for the dead as well as for the living. And when the popish priest lifts up this wafer and lays it upon the altar, then, (so they tell us), the Lord Jesus dies again and again.

Now, in short, the whole doctrine of Rome is:

1. A palpable lie;
2. An accursed idolatry;
3. A denying of the one only sacrifice of Christ.

Rome anathematizes all, according to the report of the council of Trent, who do not assent to and approve of this abomination. But God's Word proclaims a curse upon them that deny Christ and give unto the popish host the honor due unto God alone. "By one offering he hath perfected for ever them that are sanctified," as we read in Hebrews 10:14. This one offering is not to be repeated, nor to be supplemented by the mass-priest. Every one, who has yet the slightest reverence for God and His Word, must needs loathe this Romish doctrine.

It is surprising that Rome does not teach that the water in baptism is transformed into the blood of Christ. Would perhaps the falsity be then too apparent? Well then, as true as it is that the water in baptism is not transformed, so true is it that the bread and wine are not transformed in the Lord's Supper. Bread remains bread, and wine remains wine. According to His human nature, Christ is in heaven, and remains there; but, by means of the elements in the Lord's Supper which He Himself instituted, He is pleased to cause His people to experience His spiritual presence; and so greatly strengthen their faith by the eating of the bread and the drinking of the wine, that they embrace and appropriate Him as the sole cause of their salvation. The partaking of the Lord's Supper, therefore, depends upon one's possessing faith. He who is devoid of faith, cannot keep the Supper of the Lord, although he eat bread and drink wine.

Let each examine himself before he partakes of the Lord's Supper.

How this should be done is taught in . . .

Qu. 61: *After what manner must you examine yourself before you come to the Lord's Supper?*

Answer: 1. I must examine whether I abhor myself for my sins, and humble myself before God on account of them.

2. Whether I believe and trust that all my sins are forgiven me for Christ's sake.

3. Whether I also have a sincere resolution henceforward, to walk in all good works.

Such a self-examination is essential before we come to the Lord's Supper, for the very reason that it is by faith alone that Christ, in the Supper, can be partaken of. An unconverted person has no part in the Lord's Supper, even if he is a confessing member of the church. "He eateth and drinketh damnation to himself," I Cor. 11:29. How dreadful is the truth of Art. 35 of our Confession of Faith, where it states: "The ungodly indeed receives the sacrament to his condemnation, but he doth not receive the truth of the sacrament. As Judas and Simon the sorcerer both indeed received the sacrament, but not Christ, who was signified by it, of whom believers only are made partakers." O, let every one examine himself before he comes to the Lord's Supper, that Christ say not unto us, "Friend, how camest thou in hither not having a wedding garment?" For he who is not clothed with a wedding garment, did indeed climb up some other way, as a thief and a robber. The Lord shall cast him out. Baptism and confession do not constitute a ground for partaking of the Lord's Supper; it is given for God's people alone. Let every one examine himself. The key of God's Word excludes the unconverted. In the true preaching of the Word, the touchstone is given whereby every one is to try himself. Neither pastor, nor elders, may refuse to admit any to the Lord's Supper whom they consider to be unconverted, provided they are beyond reproach in life and doctrine. As concerns the state of the heart, let every one examine himself. When persons, however, behave wickedly in life and doctrine, it then becomes a different matter.

Qu. 62: *May those be admitted to the Lord's Supper, who teach false doctrines, or lead offensive lives?*

Answer: No; lest the covenant of God be profaned, and His wrath kindled against the whole church.

God's Covenant is holy; also the revealing of the same. Therefore, they who behave wickedly in life and doctrine, must be barred. When Achan had stolen of the loot of Jericho, it was for his sake that God's holy displeasure rested upon the assembly of Israel. That one man, Achan, was the accursed offender in the camp, and had to be banished. And unto the Church, the Lord has given two keys, which the consistory may not allow to become rusty, viz., the preaching of the Word, and Christian discipline. The latter is applicable to both life and doctrine, to remove out of the midst those who are publicly offensive, and deny them admittance to the Lord's Supper.

If this is not done, God's wrath is kindled over the whole church. Therefore our God-fearing forefathers refused to partake of the Supper with the Remonstrants, although the authorities persecuted them for their refusal.

Qu. 63 : *How must we then deal with such persons?*

Answer :   According to the appointment given us by Christ, Matt. 18:15-17, "If thy brother shall trespass against thee, go and tell him his fault between thee and him alone; if he shall hear thee, thou hast gained thy brother; but if he will not hear thee, then take with thee one or two more, that in the mouth of two or three witnesses every word may be established; and if he shall neglect to hear them, tell it unto the church; but if he neglect to hear the church, let him be unto thee as an heathen man and a publican."

In the ministration of discipline, the church always has to distinguish between:

PUBLIC AND . . . SECRET SINS.

This method is followed therefore in the Church Order of the Synod of Dort. This you can read in Art. 72-78. A secret sin is one of such a character, that it gave no public offense; it is known only to a single member of the congregation. For instance: Two people are working together, and one of them curses. What then is the other supposed to do? Trumpet forth the evil which such a one has committed? Alas! that happens altogether too often. Then, however, he makes himself guilty, and exposes himself to censure. The Lord says, "Go and tell him his fault between thee and him *alone*." No one else is to know ought of it at all. But if the member in question refuses to listen, and persists in his wickedness, then take one or two witnesses with you: people who likewise can keep things to themselves. Should the person concerned confess his wrong, and discontinue the same, you have gained your brother, and are obliged to forgive him. In case, however, he remains obstinate, and perseveres in the evil, then. . .and not before . . .the consistory is to be informed of the matter. Prior to this the consistory does not interfere in any affairs regarding secret sin. By refusing to listen to the admonitions, the sin has become public.

Regarding sins of a public character, the consistory first of all admonishes the offender; if he despises this admonition, censure is applied. Censure consists of three steps. In the first step the congregation is informed only of the sin committed; in the second step the name of the person is announced; thereafter follows excommunication. Before applying the second step of censure, the consistory is to request the advice of Classis.

The primary purpose of church discipline is to bring the offender to repentance. As soon, therefore, as he confesses and leaves his sin, mercy should be shown unto him. Censure is not a judicial sentence, but a medicine, a means to restore. It is not therefore imposed for a prescribed period, as for instance six weeks or three months, but until repentance is evident, and a confession is forthcoming, for which the following rule applies: Secret sins must be confessed in secret; whereas sins which are, or have become, of a public character, must be confessed in public.

The Lord cause us to walk in His Word with all due caution, lest church discipline befall us. Fear excommunication.

Smytegeldt once said that it were better for one to die on the gallows, than to be excommunicated and excluded from the Kingdom of heaven.

PART XI

The Necessity of Good Works

QUESTIONS 64-69

Parts XI and XII of this exposition are devoted to the third head of the Compendium, viz., that of *gratitude*. This third head speaks of the *law* and of *prayer*. The Ten Commandments are not spoken of separately in the Compendium, as is done in the Heidelberg Catechism; therefore the part which speaks of Gratitude is considerably shorter in the Compendium than it is in the Catechism. Whereas the Heidelberger devotes 21 Lord's Days, comprising 44 Questions, to Thankfulness, the Compendium gives but 11 Questions to this third head. In them also we are directed to the law, as the rule of life for the people of God.

First of all the *necessity* of good works is shown.

Qu. 64: *Since we are saved merely of grace through Christ, why must we then yet do good works?*

Answer: Not to merit heaven thereby, (which Christ has done), but because this is commanded me of God.

Good works are a *necessity;* those delivered by Christ *must* perform them. Not however, to merit heaven thereby. That has been accomplished by Christ, and by Him alone. As grounds for salvation good works do not count. In the justification of a sinner before God, they are of no value whatever; no, not in the very least imaginable way. But in sanctification they are indispensable. Faith without works is therefore dead, (James 2:17, 26). Faith works by love, (Gal. 5:6). The Lord exhorts His people in Matt. 5:16, "Let your light so shine before men, that they may see your good works, and glorify your Father which is in heaven."

Christ gave Himself, that He might purify unto Himself a peculiar people, zealous of good works, (Titus 2:14). Good works are therefore *requisite;* they who are delivered by Christ's blood and Spirit, *must needs* perform good works. That flows from their election: their being chosen by the Father, (Eph. 1:4); from

128

their being purchased with Christ's blood, (Titus 2:14) ; and from the renewing of the Spirit, (I Thess. 5:23). We hope to return to this however, when dealing with Qu. 66.

But those good works *do not merit*. We insist on this in opposition to Rome. God's people are saved by grace, and not of works. And if by grace, then is it no more of works, (Rom. 11: 6). Regarding meriting, grace and works exclude each other. Whereas God is pleased to reward good works, it does not signify that they merit aught at all.

Yet there is a rewarding according to merit, and by grace.

The laborers, who had worked the whole day in the vineyard, received the wages they *earned,* and for which they had bargained in the morning. But the laborers which entered the vineyard later in the day did not earn the penny which they received. The Lord of the vineyard gave them a reward of mercy. Such is the rewarding of good works. It is not given according to merit, but of grace. This caused David to say : In the keeping of Thy commandments is great reward. Of this reward of mercy is spoken also in Rev. 14:13, "and their works do follow them." This reward admits of no merit. Our works do not merit.

And if Rome slanders us, as if we did not consider good works essential as the fruit of faith, then we can cast this unwarranted scorn aside, and teach with the instructor that those delivered by Christ must needs perform good works by virtue of the renewing of their heart. Therefore we do good works, but not to merit by them, (for what can we merit?) nay, we are beholden to God for the good works we do, and not He to us, (Art. 24, Conf. of Faith).

Qu. 65 : *What purpose then do your good works answer?*

Answer: That I may thereby testify my thankfulness to God for all His benefits, and that He may be glorified by me; and that also I may be assured of the sincerity of my faith, by good works, as the fruits thereof, and that my neighbors may be edified thereby and gained to Christ.

Good works, therefore, serve:

1. Unto God's glory;

2. Unto assurance of faith;

3. Unto edification of my neighbor.

In these three purposes there is absolutely nothing said about what we should render unto God. True gratitude is therefore not a recompensing unto God for benefits received from Him; neither any payment of debt. Thus we cannot give anything unto the Lord with our good works. But He is pleased to glorify Himself in His people, and, as we read in Isa. 43:21, "This people have I formed for myself; they shall show forth my praise." And they themselves obtain the fruit thereof . . .

THE ASSURANCE OF FAITH

Sins make a separation between God and His people: they cause great darkness to cover their souls, and deprive them of the joy of faith.

But Abraham, says James, was justified by works. This does not imply however, that the Father of the faithful was declared righteous before God because of his works, but that he was assured of his righteousness by the fruit of faith. Unto this assurance of faith therefore do good works serve, (2 Peter 1:10).

Also, thirdly, with regard to our neighbor are good works necessary. The whole world has an eye on the people of God. If they can but lay one finger on that people, they blaspheme God and His work. Therefore Peter exhorts us in I Peter 2:12, "Having your conversation honest among the Gentiles: that, whereas they speak against you as evildoers, they may by your good works, which they shall behold, glorify God in the day of visitation." By good works the blasphemer is put to shame. God grant that he might by them be won unto Christ.

Although good works are absolutely without merit, nevertheless they are necessary.

Qu. 66: *Shall they also be saved who do no good works?*

Answer: No; for the Scripture says, that neither fornicators, idolaters, nor adulterers, nor whoremongers, nor thieves, nor covetous, nor drunkards, nor revilers, nor robbers, nor such like, shall inherit the kingdom of God, I Cor. 6:9, 10, unless they turn to the Lord.

This is diametrically opposed to all Antinomians. Some of them may sanction a preaching of the law, but only as a promise and a stimulant, not as God's demand. Others reject the law completely. According to them it is to be included with the Covenant of Works, and not with the Covenant of Grace. They even go to such an extreme in their wickedness, that they imply the committing of sin to be the means of magnifying grace, and deem the corruptions of their heart as an acceptable savor and taste. They say, (as Paul was slanderously reported to have said, Rom. 3:8; 6:1), "Let us continue in sin, that grace may abound." They call the flesh the old Adam, which may sin to heart's content. Paul concludes these wicked ones to be in God's righteous judgment, saying, ". . .whose damnation is just," (Rom. 3:8). In Rom. 6:1, 2, Paul also rejects completely the doctrine of the Antinomians. The answer which the Compendium gives is thus founded on God's Word. They who live in sin, cannot be saved; they shall perish, (Luke 13:3). Only by a true conversion shall we escape God's judgment.

Qu. 67: *Wherein doth the conversion of man consist?*

Answer: In a hearty repentance, and avoiding of sin, and in an earnest desire after, and doing all good works.

True conversion is God's work. (Acts 5:31). None shall turn to God by his own strength or volition, even though great changes in life do at times occur. Orpah, Ahab and others serve as examples of this. The Lord, however, works a true conversion. He stopped Paul on the way to Damascus. He opened the heart of Lydia. He does according to His sovereign good pleasure, irresistibly regenerating His elect, drawing them with the cords of His lovingkindness. When God has wrought conversion, then the renewed will works also. One converted by God does not continue to live in sin.

A true conversion is therefore:

(a) A returning unto God, Hosea 6:1;

(b) A having repentance, Jer. 31:19.

By grace do God's people turn again to the Lord. Scripture speaks no less than 140 times of turning or returning unto the Lord. Not as if we could do this in our own strength, but as this is the fruit of God's work in His people. When Zacchaeus was converted by Jesus, he forsook the wickedness wherein he had lived, and declared his desire after righteousness, (Luke 19: 8). God's work takes place first; conversion is not merely an amendment of our lives; it is a renewing. Instead of the thorn shall come up the fir tree, and instead of the brier, shall come up the myrtle tree, (Isaiah 55:13). But then, too, a new life flows forth from this work of God. Sin becomes a source of intense sorrow of soul. There likewise comes a hearty sorrow of sin, and a fleeing from it. Do not I hate them, O Lord, that hate thee? says David. The Lord also creates within them a delight unto all His commandments. In them God's people begin to walk, by an upright communion of faith with Christ; for good works are the fruits of faith.

Qu. 68: *What are good works?*

Answer: Only those which proceed from a true faith; are done according to the law of God, and to His glory; and not those which are founded on human institutions, or on our own imaginations.

Good works, therefore, have three characteristics:

(a) They proceed from the root of faith;
(b) They are done according to the rule of God's law; and,
(c) They purpose God's glory.

And so Rome, with its doctrine of good works, is again soundly repudiated. For concerning the nature as well as the unmeritoriousness of good works, Holy Scripture testifies against Rome. The unmeritoriousness had already been spoken of; the Compendium now speaks of the nature of good works.

First of all the instructor states that *good works proceed from faith.* Whatsoever is not of faith is sin, (Rom. 14:23), and cannot please God, (Heb. 11:6). The rich young man was devoid of this faith, and his works were not found to be perfect before God. It is only by faith that we obtain communion with Christ, and in Him that perfect conformity to the law. From Me is thy fruit found, says the Lord, (Hos. 14:8). In Christ, God's people not only obtain the propitiation of sins by faith, but also the acceptableness of their works before God. Outside of Christ, none of our works are pleasing unto God. By faith the branch receives strength from the vine, to bear fruit unto God, (John 15).

In the second place, *good works are done according to God's law.* That is the rule. O poor Roman Catholics, with their good works, which are but human inventions, and which are even contrary to God's law. The Lord says ,"In vain they do worship me, teaching for doctrines the commandments of men," (Matt. 15:9). God judges according to His holy law. By this our works shall be tried. This law becomes the rule for the life of God's people. The Lord writes it in their heart, and causes them to walk in His statutes, Jer. 31.

And, thirdly, *good works purpose God's glory.* That is quite a different thing than desiring to merit heaven. The whole thing that matters with regard to the works of man, is the frame of the heart. If God's glory is not intended, but we seek ourselves, our works are not good, even though the whole world should praise us. Think but of the Pharisees, who gave alms with the sounding of the trumpet, and loved to pray standing in the corners of the streets, to be seen of men. Their works were a stench in God's nostrils. Consequently, to the performance of good works, belongs the denying of one's self; they can be performed only in the dying of the old man and the resurrection of the new. Behold, such works become the delight of God's people, although they cannot perfectly keep God's law.

Qu. 69: *Can they, who are converted to God, perfectly keep the law?*

Answer: Not at all, but even the most holy men, as long as they are in this life, have only a small beginning of this obedience; yet so, that they with a sincere resolution begin to live not only according to some, but according to all the commandments of God, as they also constantly pray to God that they may daily increase therein.

There are people who assert that the law can indeed be kept perfectly by those who are converted to God. They are the *perfectionists.* With them our fathers waged a severe struggle. Perfectionism was advocated strongly by the Anabaptists. John Van

Leiden founded a "City of God" for perfectionists at Munster; and how he was put to shame!

In this life God's children cannot keep the law perfectly. God's Word teaches us this clearly when it relates the grievous sins of God's children, as of Noah, Lot, David, Peter and others. In James 3:2, we read, "For in many things we offend all," and in I John 1:8, "If we say that we have no sin, we deceive ourselves, and the truth is not in us." The Perfectionists are thus deceivers.

But how then are we to understand the words of I John 3:9, where we read, "Whosoever is born of God doth not commit sin," and that Paul says in Rom. 6:2, "How shall we, that are dead to sin, live any longer therein?"

Regeneration is a renewing of the whole man in all his parts; both in understanding and will. God does not make a soft spot in a stony heart, but takes the stony heart out of their flesh, and gives them a heart of flesh in its stead. He who is born of God does not commit sin. But this renewing is not perfect in the degrees thereof. There is a remainder of sin in the regenerated. Sin lives in them and brings them into captivity, (Rom. 7). It is likewise the continual experience of God's children, day by day. And they are taken captive because they watch not, and they languish in the warfare. By this they very highly offend God, yea, by it they incur a deadly guilt, (Canons V, 5, 6). For every sin is condemnable before God. But whatever horrible violence sin may exercise, nevertheless "God's seed remaineth in him," whosoever is born of God, (I John 3:9). It is the stellar promise of the Covenant of Grace, that God not only shall write the law in the hearts of His people, but also, that He shall cause them to walk in His statutes. Although they have but a small beginning of this obedience to God's law, and considered of themselves are nothing but a company of poor sinners, yet they delight in the law of God after the inward man, and, with a sincere resolution they begin to live according to all the commandments of God, following after perfection, (Phil. 3:12). Unto that they shall attain after this life, to serve God perfectly for ever.

PART XII

Of Prayer

QUESTIONS 70-74

In the third part of the Compendium, two matters are dealt
with, viz., the commandment and prayer. These two are most
intimately connected with one another. God's precepts are medi-
tated prayerfully. "O that my ways were directed to keep thy
statutes," says the poet in Ps. 119. Now the Compendium concludes with prayer. God's people are and remain a supplicating
people; an afflicted and poor people, that shall trust in the name
of the Lord. This has already been shown in Qu. 69, where the
answer states that they, who are converted to God, constantly
pray to God that they may daily increase in a life according to
the commandments of God.

Qu. 70: *To whom must we pray for this?*

Answer: Not to any creature, but to God alone, who can
help us, and will hear us for Jesus Christ's sake.

The whole service of God is comprehended in God's Holy Word
in the expression, "Calling upon the name of the Lord." So it is
written of the days of Seth, "Then began men to call upon the
name of the Lord," (Gen. 4:26). And God's people are entitled,
"They who call upon His Name." On the other hand, it is written
of the wicked, "They do not call upon the Lord." Yea, of His
people the faithful Jehovah complains, "Thou hast not called upon
Me, O Jacob." It appertains unto the Lord that He and He only
be called upon in prayer. It is His honor. Whosoever directs
himself in prayer to any creature, even though it were an angel
or one of the saints, offends the glory of God. He alone can
help us, and He will hear His people for Christ's sake. Christ is
the ground for the hearing of prayer, and for His sake the Lord
says, "Call upon me in the day of trouble. I will deliver thee,
and thou shalt glorify Me," (Ps. 50:15). Through Him alone
do we have access to God's throne of grace.

135

Qu. 71: *In whose name must we pray to God?*

Answer: Only in the name of Christ, (John 16:23), and not in the name of any saints.

Rome calls upon the saints. In their blindness, the Papists fall on their knees before images, and cry: "Blessed Mary; . . . . Blessed Peter. . . . .John, etc., etc., . . .pray for us." But not *one* saint in heaven can pray for us.

In the first place, the honor appertaineth not unto them, to be called upon. When the Apostle John fell down before the feet of the angel to worship him, he said, "See thou do it not: for I am thy fellowservant, and of thy brethren the prophets, and of them which keep the sayings of this book: worship God."

The holy angel hereby declared that neither he nor any other creature was to be worshiped. This honor belongs to God alone. Rome tramples God's honor under foot, and dishonors the saints, instead of honoring them.

Furthermore, as we see in the second place, the saints have nothing upon which they can plead. They too were lost sinners, who were saved only by grace, because of the merits of Christ's suffering and death.

And, thirdly, the saints in heaven cannot hear us. "Abraham is ignorant of us, and Israel acknowledges us not," (Isa. 63.16). We have no access unto God, except through the one only Mediator and Advocate Jesus Christ, Who has loved His elect unto the end. He alone is the altar before the face of God, upon which our supplications can be laid. The prayers of all saints are laid upon the golden altar of incense which is before the throne. And the smoke of the incense, which came with the prayers of the saints, ascended up before God out of the angel's hand, (Rev. 8:3, 4). No prayer is acceptable unto God, than alone in Christ. Daniel declared to have no ground in himself, saying, "We do not present our supplications before thee for our righteousnesses, but for thy great mercies," (Dan. 9:18). And those mercies are in Christ. He acquired the fulfilling of all the wants of His people; blessings are obtained through Him alone. "He shall deliver the needy when he crieth; the poor also and him that hath no helper. He shall spare the poor and needy, and shall save the souls of the needy," (Ps. 72:12, 13).

Unto Him His people have access with boldness and confidence, (Eph. 3:12). No one needs to be introduced to Him by any saint. "If then we should seek for another Mediator, who would be well affected toward us, whom could we find, who loved us more than He, Who laid down His life for us, even when we were His enemies?"

Therefore it was only through distrust that this practice of dishonoring, instead of honoring the saints, was introduced, doing that, which they never have done, nor required, but have on the contrary steadfastly rejected according to their bounden duty, as appears by their writings." (Conf. of Faith, Art. XXVI). Therefore it is not at all fitting for any to pray to God in the name of any saint, but only in the name of the Lord Jesus Christ. "And if any man sin, we have an advocate with the Father, Jesus Christ the righteous," (I John 2:1). "In whom we have boldness and access with confidence by the faith of Him," (Eph. 3:12). He Himself said, "Whatsoever ye shall ask the Father in My name, He will give it you," (John 16:23).

Qu. 72: *What must we pray to God for?*

Answer: For all things necessary for soul and body, which Christ our Lord has comprised in the prayer, He Himself has taught us.

Christ purchased both soul and body of His people, and He delivers both out of the power of sin, that soul and body shall once be with Him in everlasting glory.

For that purpose He is pleased to provide all things necessary according to soul and body. And this He provides, not because of, but upon prayer. The Lord does not need to be informed by us of all our necessities, as if He knew them not. The Lord knows what we need better than we ourselves ever could know it. But it has pleased Him to ordain and to work prayer, in which God's people exercise an active fellowship with the Lord, and wholly surrender and entrust themselves to Him in holy soul activities. No matter is too great, neither any too small, for which to seek God in prayer. Still a proper supplicating is not a requesting everything that we desire to possess. A true supplicant submits himself altogether to the will of God!

The Lord does according to His good pleasure. Consequently all prayer is to none effect which is made for the lusts of the flesh, or for the success of the wicked. Neither may any prayer be made for the dead; their lot is determined; the saints in heaven have no need for prayer, as their wants are everlastingly and perfectly filled; and for the damned all prayer is cut off.

Here again the Papists act contrary to God's will. In denying the one perfect sacrifice of Christ, they dream of a purgatory, out of which the souls must yet be delivered; consequently they offer many prayers for the dead. But such praying is not at all proper. Prayer concerns our life, and that of our neighbor, here on earth, for all needs according to both the soul and the body.

The Lord made one exception to this however, viz., for those who have sinned the sin against the Holy Ghost. That is one sin that shall not be forgiven, (Matt. 12:31, 32). "I do not say that he shall pray for it," (I John 5:16). Neither does he who commits this sin have any need of prayer; he sins presumptuously, and hardens himself in the evil. They who are beset with fears of having committed this sin, are themselves the evidence, that they are not guilty of it. God removes prayer forever from those who commit this sin.

But other than these, no sinner is too wicked to pray for his conversion and ask for the forgiveness of his sins. Stephen prayed for the very men who stoned him, saying, "Lord, lay not this sin to their charge," (Acts 7:60). And the Lord heard his prayer, as is shown by the conversion of Saul, at whose feet the clothes of the witnesses were laid.

All perhaps are acquainted also with the historical narrative of Monica, how this pious mother implored God with many fervent prayers for the conversion of her son Augustine, when he had wholly departed from the good instruction received, and degenerated in licentiousness and sinful passions. An encouraging word, spoken by Ambrose to this God-fearing mother, was fulfilled, viz., that a child of such prayers could not perish. In due season it pleased God to deliver Augustine out of sin, and raise him to be the greatest and most renowned and influential of the church-fathers. He died in the year 430. These examples show plainly that God gives confidence and boldness to pray for the salvation of even "the chief of sinners"; but in such a manner that God's honor and glory is intended above all else, and resting on the righteousness of Christ alone, who is the only ground upon which God can and will hear and answer us.

The prayer which the Lord Himself taught His disciples was to this end.

Qu. 73: *What are the words of that prayer?*

Answer: "Our Father which art in heaven, hallowed be thy name. Thy kingdom come. Thy will be done on earth, as it is in heaven. Give us this day our daily bread. And forgive us our debts, as we forgive our debtors. And lead us not into temptation, but deliver us from evil. For thine is the kingdom, and the power, and the glory, forever. Amen."

The Lord Jesus gave this prayer unto His disciples on two occasions: in Matt. 6:9, and in Luke 11:2.

In Matthew 6, the Lord admonished His disciples not to pray as the hypocrites do; for they love to pray standing in the synagogues and in the corners of the streets, that they may be seen of men. Therefore the Lord said, "Enter into thy closet." Neither use vain repetitions, as the heathen do, Christ spake further. Then He taught His disciples the "Lord's Prayer."

In Luke 11, it is written that the Lord was praying in a certain place. When He ceased, one of His disciples said unto Him, "Lord, teach us to pray, as John also taught his disciples." It was then that this same prayer was given by the Lord.

This prayer then gives the rule to be used in praying. The Lord did not prescribe it however, with this purpose that only the words of this prayer were to be used, and forbidding all others: far from it! The distress of the soul constrains God's people to call upon the Lord in their own words. Neither do the *words* of th "Lord's Prayer" have any greater virtue of themselves to be heard than those of another prayer. But that which is of primary significance is the frame of the heart. The prayer of the publican was not a long prayer, neither a formulary prayer; yet the Lord heard it. The same applies also to the prayer of the thief on the cross. The virtue of prayer lies not in the words, but in the faith by which he who prays draws nigh to God in Christ.

Formulary prayers, however, are not to be condemned. There are also formulary prayers to be used in church services, as for instance, in the Form for the Administration of Baptism, and the Form for the Administration of the Lord's Supper. Comrie stated in his writings that he always used these prayers with much edification.

And who would venture to deny the profitable guidance which lies in these prayers? And the prayer given by the Lord Jesus stands far above all those ecclesiastical prayers. If only it doesn't become customary to merely recite the "Lord's Prayer." All prayers by rote are dead.

O, how indispensable it is for us, that the Spirit of grace and of supplication teach us to pray and continually fill us with an actual need to draw nigh unto God.

In the beginning of this prayer, the Lord impresses the majesty of God upon our hearts. And when one is in a proper frame when engaged in prayer, he will abase himself in the dust before God's majesty, and cry *out of the depths*, (Ps. 130). Abraham, the father of the faithful, gave an example thereof, when with profound reverence and childlike confidence of faith, he said, "Behold now I have taken upon me to speak unto the Lord, which am but dust and ashes," (Gen. 18:27).

The prayer that the Lord taught His disciples comprises:

1st. The address, "Our Father which art in heaven;"

2nd. Six petitions, and,

3rd. The conclusion, "For thine is the kingdom, and the power, and the glory, forever. Amen."

Of the six petitions, three are designed to the glory of God, and three to our needs. The first group of three petitions asks for the hallowing of God's Name; the coming of His Kingdom, and the doing of His will. The second three supplicate for *our* daily bread; for the forgiveness of *our* sins, and for *our* preservation. How clearly is this spoken of in . . .

Qu. 74: *What do you desire of God in this prayer?*

Answer: 1. That all things which tend to the glory of God, may be promoted, and whatsoever is repugnant thereto or contrary to His will, may be prevented. 2. That He may provide me with all things necessary for the body; and as to my soul, preserve me from all evil, which might in any wise be detrimental to my salvation. Amen.

In the first three petitions the desire is expressed that all things which tend to the glory of God may be promoted. This in the first place is the *hallowing of God's Name.* By regenerating grace, a people is born that loves God's Name and seeks His glory. In the Name is the revelation of His Being. God gave unto Himself significant names, that His people may know Him and hallow Him. It is for this hallowing of God's Name that the people of the Lord ask, that they may know Him aright, with a spiritual, supernatural knowledge, which the creature does not have by nature. God glorifies this Name in His Kingdom. That Kingdom is not of this world; it is spiritual and celestial. God's Kingdom comes and increases despite the fiercest opposition, and through all tribulation. The elect are gathered in, and the victory is of the Lord. It is upon this that the Lord desires to have His people set their hearts, and not upon the world. Thus they shall do His will: the will of His command so that the will of His decree be performed in them, unto their salvation.

In this prayer the Lord also gives unto His people liberty to seek of Him the satisfying of all their needs according to soul and body. He purchased both, and is desirous to supply all their need in the manifestation of His eternal love. But there is *forgiveness* with God, that He may be feared. And as the adversary goes about as a roaring lion, He will keep them in the hour of temptation, and lead them. His Name is a strong tower, into which the righteous shall run. Throughout this prayer, the Lord Jesus teaches that the sincere supplicant seeks God's glory above all else. The first petition is for the hallowing of God's Name; the address in filial trust, and the conclusion an acknowledging that "Thine is the kingdom, and the power, and the glory, forever."

The Lord teach us to pray, as is written of Paul, "Behold, he prayeth"; and He give unto His people to live a prayerful life, that they may once praise Him forever. AMEN.